EATING AND DRINKING IN

Latin America

Featuring the foods, beverages,
dining specialties and customs of:

Argentina	Guatemala
Bolivia	Honduras
Brazil	Mexico
Chile	Nicaragua
Colombia	Panama
Costa Rica	Paraguay
Cuba	Peru
Dominican Republic	Puerto Rico
Ecuador	Uruguay
El Salvador	Venezuela

Andy Herbach

Europe Made Easy
Travel Guides

www.eatndrink.com

ISBN-13: 978-1976333743
ISBN-10: 1976333741

ACKNOWLEDGMENTS
Contributor: Karl Raaum
English editor: Marian Modesta Olson
Portuguese editor: Prof. Bryan Kennedy
Illustrations by Michael Dillon/McDill Design

ABOUT THE AUTHOR
Andy Herbach is the author of the *Eating & Drinking* series of menu translators and restaurant guides, including *Eating & Drinking in Paris*, *Eating & Drinking in Italy*, and *Eating & Drinking in Spain and Portugal*. He is also the author of several travel guides, including *Europe Made Easy*, *Paris Made Easy*, *Amsterdam Made Easy*, *Berlin Made Easy*, *Barcelona Made Easy* and *Open Road's Best of the French Riviera and Provence*. Andy is a lawyer and resides in Palm Springs, California.

You can e-mail him corrections, additions, and comments at eatndrink@aol.com or through his website at www.eatndrink.com.

Table of Contents

EATING AND DRINKING IN

Latin America

In North America, we
generally tend to identify
Latin American food
as Mexican. This is
an understandable
misconception,
as we're most
familiar with
Mexican food.
But Latin American
cuisine is extremely varied: It's tropical (especially
its assortment of delicious fruits); it's been influenced by
Africa, as a result of the West African slave trade; and it's
native Indian. Latin America is nearly three times larger
than the United States. From Mexico's deserts to the bitter
cold of the Andes to the rainforests of Central and South
America, these great differences in geography have created
a vast diversity of cuisines, making Latin America one of
the world's most interesting destinations for food lovers.

If you love to travel as we do, you know the importance of
a good guide. The same is true of dining. A good guide can
make all the difference between a memorable evening and a
nightmare, or even a dull one, but who wants a dull evening
when you're on vacation? This book will help you find your
way around a menu that is written in Spanish or Portuguese.
Instead of fumbling with a bulky, conspicuous travel guide
(most of which usually include a very incomplete listing of
foods), this small book is an alphabetical listing of food and
drink commonly found on menus in Latin America.

Traveling to a foreign country means something different to
everyone. For every vacation there are different expectations,
different needs, and every traveler has his or her own idea of

what will make that vacation memorable. For us, the making of a memorable vacation begins and ends with food. Beyond the simple pleasures of eating, dining in Latin America gives you an insight into the soul of its people. It's a glimpse of their customs, their likes and dislikes, their foibles, their accomplishments.

If your idea of a vacation is an all-inclusive resort, you may not need this book. (Not that we have any objection to vacations of this nature; we don't, and in fact, we would happily leave on one right this instant, if the opportunity presented itself!) We are not the most adventurous people in the world, but we do enjoy getting a taste of the culture of the country we are visiting. We'd sooner visit a great little restaurant than a museum any day. Just as looking at pictures of Machu Picchu can be an enjoyable experience, but certainly not as incredible as actually being there, reading about the cuisine of Latin America, while informative, would not be *delicious*.

Unfortunately, even people who speak passable Spanish or Portuguese can have trouble reading a menu. Although you may know the word for meat in Spanish is *carne*, you might be surprised to discover that *ropa vieja* (which means "old clothes") on a menu is, in fact, shredded beef. This guide was created for the traveler who wants to know what is on the menu, but is afraid to, or cannot ask. We know the panic of opening a menu without recognizing one word on it and the disappointment of being served something other than what you thought you'd ordered. On our first trip overseas, when we thought we had ordered chicken, we were served a plate of cold brains.

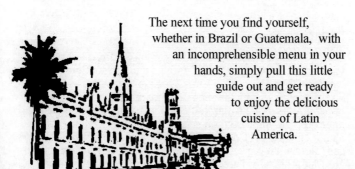

The next time you find yourself, whether in Brazil or Guatemala, with an incomprehensible menu in your hands, simply pull this little guide out and get ready to enjoy the delicious cuisine of Latin America.

South America

Argentina

Argentine cuisine can be characterized as meat, meat and
more meat! Meat dishes are often served on a small grill next
to the table. The national dishes of Argentina are frequently
a composite of Spanish and Italian food. Try the *parillada*
(mixed grill), *ñoquis* (Italian gnocchi or potato dumplings)
and *pucheros* (hearty stews). There are many versions of
chimichurri. This delicious sauce used for grilled meat and
comes in a green version (*chimichurri verde*) and a red version (*chimichurri rojo*). It's usually made of chopped parsley,
minced garlic, vegetable oil, oregano, and white vinegar.
Argentina produces world-class wines. Only France, Italy,
Spain and the United States produce more wine annually.
Dulce de leche (milk simmered with vanilla and sugar and
served over toast or *flan*) is a popular Argentine dessert.

Bolivia

Bolivian dishes are frequently rich in meat, potatoes and corn.
Lunch is frequently the main meal of the day. Hot red peppers are found in many dishes. As it is a landlocked nation,
seafood is not common in Bolivia although trout from Lake
Titicaca appears on menus. Soups are often complete meals
and loaded with vegetables, meat, potatoes, and *quinua* (a
rice-like grain). Try the ever-present *chuños* (freeze-dried
potatoes), *empanada salteña* (ground meat with pepper, hot
sauce, chicken, diced potatoes, olives and raisins wrapped in
dough, then baked), *fricassé* (pork cooked in a spicy sauce
and served with potatoes and corn) and *sopa de maní* (roasted-peanut soup). For the daring, try *chicha*. This grain alcohol
is made by chewing corn, spitting it out, adding water and
allowing the mixture to ferment. It's sweet and can be very
potent. We skipped the *ají de lengua* (cow's tongue in a chili
sauce).

Brazil

Brazil is a large country, nearly half of the South American
territory. It's home to over half of the population of South
America. As a result, its cuisine is regional and diverse. Brazil
is a melting pot: from the seafood of its coastal regions, to the
tropical fruits of the Amazon, to the international flair of the
large cities, to the food of the southern regions, influenced
by not only the cold climate, but the large number of Italian
and German immigrants. Portuguese explorers arrived here in
the 16th century and greatly influenced its cuisine. The food
found in Brazil is also influenced by native Indians, Africans,
Syrians, Lebanese and Asians. The largest populations of
Japanese outside of Japan is found here.

Black beans (*feijão preto*) are an important part of Brazilian cuisine, from simple dishes such as black beans and rice to *feijoada* (a stew of meats and black beans). Originally, this national dish was made from scraps; today, it can be found in sophisticated restaurants.

Inexpensive eateries, especially street vendors, serve turnovers (*empadinhas*) filled with everything from meat to fruit. Seafood, especially in coastal areas, is featured on many menus. The Portuguese brought *balcalhau* (salt cod), and there are said to be as many ways to make salt cod as days in a year.

Roasted meats can be found at a *churrascaria*. Pork, chicken and beef are cooked over an open fire and servers walk around with large plat-ters of the meat which is sliced at your table.

Many dishes are thickened with *manioc*, also called cassava root or yuca. *Dendê* is a palm oil (with a high saturated fat content), used in small amounts to season a variety of dishes.

Brazilian dishes often feature wonderful tropical fruits. Papaya, mango, bananas and especially coconut serve as side dishes and as the basis for great desserts.

For the adventurous, try *chachaça*, a potent alcoholic beverage made from sugar cane. Brazil is also known for delicious, strong coffee such as *cafezhino*.

Chile

The cuisine of Chile is quite international, and its wines are respected the world over. Because of Chile's long coastline, seafood is abundant. *Albacora* (swordfish), *corvina* (sea bass) and *chupe de mariscos* (seafood stew) are only a few of the seafood dishes you'll find here. The beef in Chile, while quite good, is generally not considered to be of the same quality as in Argentina and Uruguay. *Curanto* (a dish of meat, often suckling pig, vegetables and seafood) and *cazuela* (the Chilean version is thick and includes meat, potatoes and corn) are two of the hearty soups found here. In the late afternoon, tea time, called "*once*," is popular. Similar to the British "elevenses," tea or coffee is served with cookies, toast, cheese or other small appetizers. *Once* means eleven and *aguardiente* (the national "fire water") has eleven letters. So when someone says that he is having his "*once*," it may also mean that he is having a drink of *aguardiente*.

Colombia

Colombian food varies greatly by region, from seafood soups of the coast to *ajiaco bogotano* (thick potato and chicken soup) found in the capital to the tropical fruits of the interior. Colombians eat large and spicy evening meals. Breakfast and lunch are generally light meals. *Arroz con pollo* (rice and chicken) is found on almost every menu. Try *puchero bogotano* (boiled vegetables, meat and potatoes), *piquete* (meat, vegetables and potatoes in a hot-pepper sauce) and *bandeja paisa*, also called *plato montañero,* (a dish with ground beef, sausage, salt pork, beans, rice, avocado and fried egg). For dessert, try *obleas* (large frosted wafers), and don't forget that Colombia is famous for its rich coffee.

Ecuador

Ecuador is known for its seafood (especially shrimp and lobster), exotic tropical fruits and interesting potato dishes. Try *llapingachos* (mashed potatoes with cheese), *locro* (a corn or potato soup with cheese and avocados) and *yaguarlocro* (potato soup with blood sausage). Coastal cuisine features dishes such as *arroz con menestra* (white rice with black beans or lentils) and *patacones* (fried plantains). As in parts of Colombia, you can still find *cuy* on the menu. We'll pass; it's grilled guinea pig.

Paraguay

Paraguayan restaurants feature beef (especially the mixed charcoal grill of meats called *parrillada*), pasta and *empanadas* (turnovers filled with various ingredients). Try the national dishes of *sooyosopy* (soup of cornmeal and ground meat, usually served with rice) and *sopa paraguaya* ("Paraguayan soup" of mashed corn bread, cheese, onion, milk and eggs). The national "fire water" is *caña*, an alcoholic beverage made from sugar cane and similar to rum. Paraguay is an international destination for fishing, and Paraguay's rivers contain unusual fish such as *surubi*, a fresh-water fish similar to catfish. For dessert try *dulce de leche* (milk simmered with vanilla and sugar and served over toast or *flan*) and delicious fruits such as papaya, pineapple and melons.

Peru

As a result of its diverse geography (from the Andes mountains to the Amazon) and from Spanish, indigenous Indian, Asian and African influences, Peruvian cuisine is an eclectic mix. Seafood dominates in coastal areas. Pepper and garlic are popular and found in many dishes, making Peruvian cuisine occasionally extremely hot. Vegetables and tropical fruits are abundant. Try *ají de gallina* (shredded chicken in a cream and pepper sauce), *lomo saltado* (stir-fried steak served with onions, rice, tomatoes and vegetables) and *pisco* (a colorless and potent alcoholic beverage made from corn or grapes). Because of the large Asian population in Peru, you'll find many Chinese restaurants or *chifas*.

Uruguay

Although one of the smallest countries in South America, Uruguay is quite cosmopolitan. Half of its citizens reside in the capital city, and they are mainly of Spanish, Portuguese and Italian desent. Lunch is often a large and long meal in Uruguay. Beef dominates the cuisine. Dinner is almost always served extremely late. Don't miss *carbonada* (beef stew, usually with rice, pears, peaches and raisins), *chivito al plato* (steak topped with a fried egg and served with potato salad, a green salad and french fries), *milanesa* (breaded and fried veal cutlet), *morcilla dulce* (sweet blood sausage) and *olímpicos* (club sandwiches). For desert, you'll love *alfajores* (shortbread cookies filled with *dulce de leche* and covered with chocolate).

Venezuela

From cosmopolitan Caracas to small Andean villages to Caribbean coastal towns, Venezuela has much to offer the food lover. Venezuelan cuisine is quite international. You'll find steaks, seafood, many Italian restaurants and a Caribbean influence. Try *parrilla criolla* (marinated beef cooked on a grill), *pasticho* (a dish very similar to lasagna), *sancocho* (vegetable soup with meat or fish), *hallaca* (meat and any number of ingredients and spices stuffed in dough, then wrapped in banana leaves and boiled in water) and *muchacho* (beef loin roasted and served in a sauce). Skip the *lapa*; it's a large roasted rodent and on the endangered species list. For dessert, try the delicious *bien me sabe* (cake with coconut cream topping).

Tipping in South America
Always check your bill to determine if service (*servicio*) is included. For a quick reference to tipping in South America, see page 16.

Mealtimes
Breakfast tends to be light, especially in Argentina, since dinner is eaten quite late (rarely before 9:00 p.m). Brazilians dine very late. Few eat dinner before 9:00 p.m., and if you arrive at a restaurant early, you'll be dining with other tourists. Lunch is sometimes the main meal of the day in Chile and in Ecuador.

Water
Most larger cities in South America have adequate tap water.

Such is not the case in areas outside of major cities. Don't drink the water anywhere in Ecuador. Salmonella is also a concern in outlying areas, so make sure your meats and eggs are thoroughly cooked ("*bien cocido*" in Spanish and "*bem passado*" in Portuguese). We prefer to play it safe and drink only mineral water. Many foods and drinks may have been made or washed with contaminated water, such as fruit juices made from concentrate or salads and fruits. Peeled fruits are the safest. And the ice in your cocktail: Was it made from tap water? Make sure that the water used for tea and coffee has been adequately boiled. It is not unknown for unscrupulous restaurant owners to fill mineral-water bottles with plain tap water. The best precaution is to make sure the bottle is sealed when it is brought to your table.

Central America

Eggs and beans (*huevos y frijoles*) are the staples of Central American cuisine. *Tortillas* (a flat, round, cooked unleavened bread) are almost always included in any meal along with *salsa picante* (hot-pepper sauce). *Comedores* (local restaurants) allow you to sample *huevos y frijoles*, usually along with cheese and meat. Remember that, if you plan on dining at a restaurant that caters to tourists, you are almost always going to spend much more money than you would at *comedores*. *Comida típica* is a basic menu found in *comedores*, and consists of meat, beans and rice.

Costa Rica

Although it's served all day long, *gallo pinto* (mixed cooked beans and rice) is the national breakfast of Costa Rica and is served everywhere. *Bocas* are appetizers served with alcoholic beverages. *Casados* (fish, meat or chicken with rice, beans and vegetables, usually served with a small salad) is a common inexpensive evening meal. It means "married." Other specialties include *guiso de maíz* (thick corn stew), *horchata* (a clear, sometimes dangerous alcoholic beverage, made from corn), *tamales* (corn-meal dough filled with meat and sauce, wrapped in a banana leaf or corn husk, and then steamed; olives, rice and raisins are often included) and *olla de carne* (beef stew usually with plantains and yucca). On the Caribbean coast, plantains and coconut find their way into many dishes.

El Salvador

Seafood (clams, oysters, lobster, shrimp, crab, corvina and robalo) dominates the cuisine of El Salvador. Strangely, despite the country's past relations with the United States, American fast food restaurants are everywhere and quite popular. Some specialties include *pupusas* (fried *tortillas* filled with cheese, beans and/or meat) that you'll find everywhere, *curtido* (spicy cole slaw), *minutas* (honey-flavored drink made with crushed ice) and *horchata* (a sweet rice-based beverage frequently served in a plastic bag).

Guatemala

If you want to sample genuine Guatemalan dishes, you'll usually find them at inexpensive *comedores* (local restaurants) that are everywhere and usually serve only *comida típica* (native food). *Boquitas* are small appetizers such as olives, peanuts or crackers. *Tuntas* (freeze-dried potatoes) are served with many dishes. Other specialties include *antojito* (*tortilla* sandwich filled with beef, tomatoes and onions), *carne guisada* (sauce with stewed beef), *chirmol* (grilled steak served with tomato and onion sauce), *chuchitos* (meat and sauce stuffed in dough and wrapped in a corn husk), *fiambre* (meat, fish and cheese salad) and *mosh* (oats with honey and cinnamon). For the true travel experience, some might want to try *tepezcuintle* (a Mayan specialty, the largest member of the rodent family).

Honduras

Comedores (local restaurants) serve *plato típico* (a combination of rice, meat, beans, cheese, *tortillas* and eggs). On the coast, inexpensive seafood is prevalent. Some Honduran specialties are *anafre* (bean paste smothered with melted cheese), *pinchos* (a dish similar to shish kebabs) and *sopa de mondongo* (tripe stew or soup). *Pupusas* (like those found in El Salvador, but almost always filled with pork) are found everywhere. *Yuca* (cassava, an edible root that yields a starch) is found in many dishes. Tropical fruits add sweetness to many dishes. Honduran rum (*ron*) is of excellent quality, and cold local beer (*cerveza*) is a great way to quench your thirst on a hot, tropical Honduran afternoon.

Nicaragua

Plato típico is a large and inexpensive meal containing any of the following: beans, rice, meat, fried plantains, *tortillas*, cheese and a salad. It's served at most inexpensive restaurants. *Gallo pinto* (mixed cooked beans and rice) is found everywhere, as are *nacatamales* (*tortillas* filled with meat, corn and sauce and steamed in banana leaves or a corn husk). Seafood is abundant near the coast and is usually served in a garlic sauce (*al ajillo*). Some other specialties are *pana de coco* (coconut bread), *tajaditas*, (fried plantain chips) and *tortillas con quesillo* (fried corn *tortillas* with melted cheese). Nicaraguans delight in a bounty of tropical fruits that, combined with milk and/or coconut, make great desserts.

Panama

According to some, Panama means "abundance of fish," so don't miss *ceviche* (raw seafood marinated in lemon and lime juice) and *corvina* (sea bass). *Langosta* (lobster) and *gambas* (shrimp) are served everywhere. The national dish is *arroz con pollo* (rice and chicken). Specialties include *ropa vieja* (rice covered with spicy shredded beef and green peppers. The term means "old clothes"), *sancocho* (a spicy stew of meat and vegetables) and *arroz con coco y titi* (rice with coconut and shrimp). For dessert try *arroz con cacao* (chocolate-flavored rice pudding).

Tipping in Central America

Tipping is extremely confusing in Central America, because it varies by country. It's typical for *impuesto de valor agregado* (IVA) to be added to your restaurant bill. This is a tax. But you must also check to see if the tip has been added. If it has, you'll see *servicio incluido* on your bill. Depending on the country you're visiting, you may still be expected to tip the waiter. See "Tips on Tipping" on page 16.

Mealtimes

Similar to the United States and Canada.

Water

We don't drink tap water unless we are absolutely sure that it's safe. The general rule is to only drink bottled water. All water must be purified in Guatemala, Honduras and (depending on whom you talk to) in El Salvador. Although water is said to be safe in the major cities of other Central American countries, why risk it?

Additional precautions are listed under "Water" in the South America and Mexico sections of this guide.

Puerto Rico

The cuisine of Puerto Rico has been influenced by Spain, the Caribbean and Africa. This combination makes Puerto Rican cuisine varied and unique. Of course, due to its commonwealth status,  the cuisine has also been influenced by the United States (which explains the unfortunate appearance of so many

American fast-food restaurants). The finest, fresh
dishes are found along Puerto Rico's 270-mile c
is island cuisine that blends European, African,
and Arawak Indian foods. Some specialties incl
(a thick stew made with rice and with meat or s
Puerto Rico's most popular native dish), *enceb*
smothered in onions), *surrullitos* (deep-fried c
stuffed with cheese) and *serenata* (fish in vine
onions, avocados and vegetables). Don't miss *tembleque*
(coconut pudding) and *cocos fríos* (chilled coconuts, tops
chopped off, drunk with a straw). No trip to Puerto Rico is
complete without *ron* (rum), the national drink.

Tipping in Puerto Rico
As in the United States, a 15% to 20% tip is expected. Service
is rarely included.

Mealtimes
Similar to mealtimes in the United States and Canada.

Water
Most people drink the tap water in Puerto Rico without prob-
lems. However, if you have a sensitive stomach, it is recommended that you drink bottled water.

Dominican Republic

The food of the Dominican
Republic is influenced by Spain,
the Caribbean and Africa
and is known for thick,
rich sauces. Outside of
resorts, international cuisine
is not common. Several noteworthy
local dishes include *arroz con habichuelas* (rice and
beans served with nearly everything), *asopao* (a thick stew
made with rice and meat or seafood, similar to the Puerto
Rican national dish of the same name), *calabaza* (a squash
served with many dishes), *cocos fríos* (chilled coconuts, tops
chopped off, drunk with a straw) and *sopa criolla dominicana* (a soup of stewed meat, greens, onions, spices and
pasta). Some of the finest lobster (*langosta*) is found here.
Plátanos (plantains) are a common side dish. Often, they are
baked and called *plátanos horneados*. Don't miss *quesillo
de leche y piña* (milk and pineapple flan).

Tipping
The tax referenced on your restaurant bill includes a 10% service charge. It is still customary to tip 10-15%

Mealtimes
Although tourist restaurants may open for dinner at 6:00 p.m.,

locals do not eat until much later, 9:00 or 10:00 p.m.

Water

Do not drink the tap water in the Dominican Republic. Be careful with salads and fruits, and read the sections of this guide discussing water in South and Central America and Mexico.

Mexico

Mexican cuisine is considered by many to be one of the world's greatest. Corn is the staple of Mexican cooking. *Tortillas*, *tacos* and *enchiladas* dominate the Mexican table. Visitors from the United States are generally familiar with Mexican food. Of course, some have the misconception that Mexican food is the same as tex-mex, which it is not. Not all Mexican food is hot, and Mexican cooks do not use chili in everything. Mexican food is a combination of local dishes and Spanish cuisine. Some Mexican specialties are *chimichangas* (deep-fried *tortillas* stuffed with beef, beans, chilies and spices), *huachinango* (red snapper), *gorditas* (small, thick *tortillas* filled with chopped meat, cheese, beans and vegetables, fried, and served with lettuce and chili sauce on top), *guacamole* (mashed avocado, tomato, onion, cilantro and chilies), *huevos rancheros* (fried eggs served with a hot tomato sauce) and *pollo borracho* (fried chicken in a tequila-based sauce). *Moles* (thick, dark complex chili sauces) vary by region. One famous mole is *mole poblano* (chicken with a delicious sauce of chili pepper, chocolate and spices).

Tipping in Mexico
In a restaurant, you should tip 15% - 20%. Remember, waiters and waitresses depend on tips, as most restaurants pay an extremely small hourly wage.

Mealtimes
Lunch is usually the largest meal of the day and is eaten between 2:00 p.m. and 4:00 p.m. Dinner is not served until 9:00 p.m. or 10:00 p.m., with the exception of restaurants in tourist areas.

What more can be said than "turista"? Don't drink the water (and remember this includes ice), be careful with salads and fruits and read the sections of this guide discussing water in South and Central America. Don't ruin your vacation by failing to follow these simple precautions.

Cuba

Cuban cuisine is a captivating mixture of African, Caribbean and Spanish influences. The food of Cuba relies on basic herbs and spices such as oregano, bay leaves, cumin and garlic. Cuban dishes are not known for creamy or heavy sauces, and few dishes are deep-fried. Meats are frequently marinated in citrus juices and roasted over a low heat until the meat falls off the bone. Meat dishes are usually accompanied by black beans (*frijoles negros*) and rice (*arroz*). *Plátanos* (a vegetable that looks like a banana, picked when green, and unlike a banana, is never eaten raw) are everywhere and are served in many ways from sweet (*plátanos dulce*) to fried (*tostones*). *Yuca* (we sometimes call this root vegetable cassava) and *boniato* (similar, but not related to a yam and sometimes called the Cuban sweet potato) are common side dishes. *Sofrito* (onion, garlic, oregano, green pepper fried in olive oil) forms the basis of many dishes.

Some Cuban specialties include *lechon asado* (pork roast), *media noche* (ham and cheese sandwich topped with mustard and pickles), *masas de puerco frito* (fried chunks of pork) and *flan* (caramel custard).

The sweet and rich desserts of Cuba often feature the wonderful tropical fruits of this island, especially coconut.

Tipping in Cuba
There are really no rules on tipping in Cuba, but you should tip at least 10% if no service charge has been added.

Water
Tap water is generally safe to drink, but bottled water, which is readily available, is recommended.

Tips on Tipping

Tipping in Latin America can be extremely confusing. This will help you figure out when to tip and what amount to tip in Latin America. Always ask if the service charge is included.

South America

Argentina: A service charge has usually been added. If not, tip 10%-15%.

Bolivia: A service charge will most likely be added to your bill. Tip an extra 10%.

Brazil: Almost always included in your bill, but be careful to check. If there is a service charge (usually 10% is included), you should leave an additional 5%. If it is not included, tip 15%.

Chile: A 10% gratuity may have been added. Add an extra 10%.

Colombia: A 10% service charge may have been added. Add 5%-10%.

Ecuador: A service charge may have been added. Tip an extra 10%.

Paraguay: A service charge may have been added. Tip an extra 10%.

Peru: A service charge is usually added to your bill. If it is, tip up to 10%. If the service charge has not been added, tip up to 15%.

Uruguay: A service charge is usually included. If not, tip 10%.

Venezuela: A service charge is usually added. Add 5-10%.

Central America

Costa Rica: 10-15%, if no service charge.
El Salvador: 10%, if no service charge.
Guatemala: 15%, if no service charge.
Honduras: 10%, if no service charge.
Nicaragua: 10%, if no service charge.
Panama: 10-15%, if no service charge.

In all Central American countries, even if there is a service charge, it is always greatly appreciated if you give the waiter an additional cash tip.

Mexico
15-20%, if no service charge.

Puerto Rico
15-20%. A service charge is rarely included in the bill.

Dominican Republic
A service charge is often included, but it is customary to tip 10-15%.

Cuba
There are really no set rules on tipping in Cuba, but you should tip at least 10% if no service charge has been added.

Types of Eating Establishments

Asador: grill room, rotisserie.

Cafetería: self-service cafeteria.

Cervecería: bar.

Comedor: dining room. Local restaurants often serving fixed-priced meals (especially in Central America, Argentina, Bolivia and Peru).

Chichería: restaurant serving local dishes (Chile).

Chifa: Chinese restaurant (Peru, Chile and Colombia).

Churrasquería: restaurant that specializes in grilled meats. These are called churrascaria in Brazil.

Confitería: teas, sandwiches and cakes (Argentina, Uruguay).

Fonda: inn (frequently serving food).

Fuentes de soda: sandwiches, tea and coffee (Chile).

Hostería: informal restaurant, usually associated with an inn.

Marisquería: seafood restaurant that frequently has tanks of live seafood.

Merendero: an open-air snack bar.

Mesón: simple, local restaurant.

Paladare: usually a family-run restaurant (Cuba).

Pardillera: restaurant that specializes in grilled meats.

Parilla: grilled and barbecued meats (Argentina, Peru and Uruguay).

Pastelería: pastry shop.

Picado/Picá: family homes serving limited menus (Chile).

Picanterías: restaurants serving local dishes (Peru).

Restaurante: We think you can figure this out.

Restaurante Particulare: usually a family-run restaurant (Cuba).

Rotisería: deli (Argentina).

Salon de té: tea room. Especially found in Chile.

Taberna: tavern.

Tasca: bar serving small snacks (*tapas*).

Tetería: tea shop.

Venta: country inn serving food.

How to Use This Guide

In Latin America, menus are often posted outside of the establishment or in a window. This makes choosing a restaurant easy and fun as you "window shop" for your next meal. (You can refer to our guide outside so you seem more informed inside.)

Remember that the dish you ordered may not be exactly as described in this guide. Every chef is (and should be) innovative. What we have listed for you is the most common version of a dish. And remember, if a menu has an English translation it does not mean that the translation is correct!

The Spanish menu-translator section of this guide includes the wonderful dishes of Spanish-speaking travel destinations such as Mexico, Central and South America, Puerto Rico, Cuba, the Dominican Republic and Spain. The Portuguese menu-translator section will help you enjoy the cuisine of Brazil.

Smoking

In Latin America, it seems that everyone, from the very young to the very old, smokes. Latin America is gradually going smoke-free. The majority of Latin American countries now ban smoking in enclosed public spaces.

Tips on Budget Dining

There is no need to spend a lot of money to have good food. There are all kinds of fabulous foods to be had inexpensively.

Eat at a neighborhood restaurant. You'll usually know the price of a meal before entering, as many eating establishments post the menu and prices in the window. Never order anything whose price is not known in advance unless you're feeling adventurous.

Delis and food stores can provide cheap and wonderful meals. Buy some cheese, bread, wine and other snacks and have a picnic. Remember to pack a corkscrew and eating utensils when you leave home.

Lunch, even at the most expensive restaurants, always has a lower price. So, have lunch as your main meal.

Restaurants that have menus written in English (especially those near tourist attractions) are almost always more expensive than neighborhood restaurants.

If you're concerned about the cost of a meal, the menu of the day is usually a better value for your money than purchasing food *á la carte*.

Street vendors generally sell inexpensive and good food. For the cost of a cup of coffee or a drink, you can linger at a café and watch the world pass you by for as long as you want. It's one of travel's greatest bargains.

There are many great markets (*mercados*) in both the small towns and large cities of Latin America where you can often find local favorites to sample. Restaurants near the markets frequently serve great meals made from the fresh foods on sale at the market.

Eat when the locals eat, drink what the locals drink and eat what the locals are eating. Your trip will be better and more interesting for it, and local favorites are generally cheaper.

And don't eat at McDonald's, for God's sake.

Buen Provecho
(Bon Appetit)

Portuguese Pronunciation Guide

If you are looking for a comprehensive guide to speaking Brazilian Portuguese, this is not the the right place. What follows is simply a few tips for speaking Portuguese and a very brief pronunciation guide. Don't try to speak Spanish in Brazil. French is the linguistic cousin to Portuguese. Words are stressed on the last syllable, but generally if a word ends with a, e or o, the stress falls on the next to the last syllable.

a like a in father or a in bang

â like ung in hung

ã a nasal "ung"

b as in English

c usually like c in cat, but followed by e or i like c in city

ç like s in sun

ch like sh in shun

d as in English

e usually like e in bet (when stressed). Sometimes like a in gate. When not stressed, like er i n mother. At the beginning of a word, like i in bit

é like e in bet

ê like a in gate

f as in English

g usually like g in good, but when followed by e or i like s in measure

h is silent

i like ee in weed

j like s in pleasure

k as in English

l as in English

lh like li in million

m like m in met. Between a vowel and a consonant or at the end of a word, it nasalizes the vowel

n as in English

nh like ny in canyon

o like o in note, oo in soon or aw in raw

ô like o in note

p as in English

q like k in kite when qui or que. Like the qu in quick when qua or quo

qü like qu in quick

r similar to h at the beginning of a word. Single tap on the roof of the mouth when in the middle of a word

rr similar to h

s like s in sit. At the end of a word, like sh. Between two vowels or before b, d, g, l, m, n, r or v, like z in zebra

ss like s in sun

t as in English

u like oo in moon

v as in English

w as in English

x has four pronunciations: ks as in explicar, sh as in xarope, z as in examinar and s as in execto

z as in English

English to Portuguese

This is a brief listing of some familiar English food and food-related words that you may need in a restaurant setting. It is followed by a list of phrases that may come in handy.

allergy, alergia

anchovy, anchova

another, um outro/mais um

appetizer, entrada

apple, maçã

artichoke, alcachofra

ashtray, cinzeiro

asparagus, espargos

bacon, bacon/toucinho

baked, no forno

banana, banana

bathroom, banho

bean, feijão

beef, boi/carne

beef steak, bife

beer, cerveja

beverages, bebida

big, grosso

bill, conta

bitter, amargo

boiled, cozido

bottle, garrafa

bowl, tigela

braised, nas brasas

bread, pão

breaded, empanado

bread roll, pãozinho

breakfast, café-da-manhã
    pequeno-almoço

broccoli, brócolis

broth, caldo

burnt, queimado

butter, manteiga

cabbage, couve

cake, bolo

calories, calorias

candle, vela

carbonated, com gas

carrot, cenoura

cash (money), dinheiro

cashier, caixa

cereal, cereal

chair, cadeira

champagne, champagne

change (coins), resto/troco

cheap, barato

check (bill), conta

cheers, saúde

cheese, queijo

cherry, cereja/acerola

chicken, frango

chocolate, chocolate

cigarette, cigarro

clams, mexilhões

closed, fechado

cod, bacalhau

coffee, café

coffee with milk, café com leite

cold, frio

corkscrew, saca-rolhas

corn, milho

cost (price), preço

cream, creme

cucumber, pepino

cutlery, talheres

cutlet, costeleta

cup, xícara/chávena

decaffeinated, descafeinado

dessert, sobremesa

diabetic, diabético

diet, alimentação/dieta
dinner (supper), jantar
dirty, sujo
dish (plate), prato
drink, bebida
dry, seco
duck, pato
egg, ovo
eggplant, berinjela
enough, suficiente
expensive, caro
fish, peixe
food, alimento
food poisoning, intoxicação
  alimentar
fork, garfo
free, grátis
french fries, batatas fritas
fresh, fresco
fried, frito
fruit, fruta
game (meat), caça
garlic, alho
gin, gin
glass, copo
goat, cabra
goose, ganso
grape, uva
grapefruit, toranja
greasy, gorduroso
green bean, vagem/feijão-verde
grilled, grelhada
half, metade
ham, presunto (smoked)/fiambre
  (cured)
hamburger, hambúrguer
hangover, ressaca
honey, mel
hors-d'oeuvre, entrada
hot, quente
ice, gelo

ice cream, sorvete/gelado
ice cube, cubo de gelo
included, incluído
juice, suco/sumo
ketchup, ketchup
knife, faca
kosher, kosher
lamb, cordeiro
large, grande
lemon, limão
less, menos
lettuce, alface
little (small), pequeno
liver, fígado
lobster, lagosta
lunch, almoço
match, fósforo
mayonnaise, maionese
meat, carne
medium (cooked), médio
melon, melão
menu, cardápio/ementa
milk, leite
mineral water, água mineral
mineral water (sparkling), água
  com gás
mixed, misto
more, mais
mushroom, cogumelo
mussel, mexilhão
mustard, mostarda
napkin, guardanapo
no, não
non-alcoholic, analcoólico
non-smoker, não-fumador
nut, noz
oil, azeite
olive oil, azeite de azeitona
olive, azeitona
omelette, omelete
onion, cebola

only, sozinho

orange, laranja

orange juice, suco de laranja

order, to, pedir

oyster, ostra

pastry, massa

peach, pêssego

peanut, amendoim

pear, pêra

peas, ervilhas

pepper (spice), pimenta

pepper (vegetable), pimento

perch, poleiro

pineapple, abacaxi/ananás

plate (dish), prato

please, por favor

plum, ameixa

pork, porco

potato, batata

poultry, aves

prawn, camarão (camarões)

quail, codorniz

quick, rápido

rabbit, coelho

rare, mal passado

raspberry, framboesa

raw, crú

receipt, recibo

reservation, reserva

restroom, toilette/banheiro

rice, arroz

roast, assado

roll, salgadinho/rissól

rum, cachaça

salad, salada

salad dressing, tempero da salada

salmon, salmão

salt, sal

sandwich, sanduíche/sandes

sauce, molho

sausage, salsicha

scrambled eggs, ovos mexidos

seafood, fruto do mar

service, serviço

shellfish, mariscos

shrimp, camarão (camarões)

small, pequeno

smoked, defumado

smoke, fumo

snails, caracóis

sole, linguado

soup, sopa

sour, azedo

spaghetti, espaguete

sparkling, espumante

specialty, especialidade

spicy, picante

spinach, espinafre

spoon, colher

stale (bread), duro

steak, bife

steam, vapor

stew, picadinho/estufado

straw (drinking), canudinho/
palhinha

strawberry, morango

sugar, açúcar

sugar substitute, adoçante

supper, jantar

sweet, doce

table, mesa

tea, chá

tea with lemon, chá com limão

tea with milk, chá com leite

teaspoon, colher de chá

temperature, temperatura

thank you, obrigado (masculine)
obrigada (spoken by a woman)

tip, gorjeta

toasted, torrado

tomato, tomate

tonic, tônica

toothpick, palito
translation, tradução
trout, truta
tuna, atum
turkey, perú
undercooked (rare), mal passado
veal, vitela
vegetables, verduras/legumes/
   hortaliças
vegetarian, vegetariano (for a
   man)/vegetariana (for a woman)
venison, carne de veado
vinegar, vinagre
waiter, garçon
waitress, garconete
water, água
watermelon, melancia
well done, bem passado
wine, vinho
wine list, lista dos vinhos
wine (red), vinho tinto
wine (rosé), vinho rosé
wine (sparkling), vinho espumante
wine (white), vinho branco
with, com
without, sem
yes, sim
yogurt, iogurte
zucchini, abobrinha

Helpful Phrases

please, por favor
thank you, obrigado

good morning, bom dia
good afternoon, boa tarde
good evening, boa noite
good night, boa noite
goodbye, adeus/tchau

hello, olá
hi, oi

I am sorry., Desculpe./Perdão.

Do you speak English?, Fala
   inglês?
I don't speak Portuguese., Não
   falo português.

excuse me, com licença
I don't understand., Não percebo.

I'd like, Queria
a table, uma mesa
I'd like to make a reservation.,
   Queria fazer uma reserva.
for one, para um/uma
for two, para dois
   três (3), quatro (4), cinco (5),
      seis (6), sete (7), oito (8),
      nove (9), dez (10)
now, agora
today, hoje
this evening, hoje à noite
tomorrow, amanhã

near the window, pero da janela
outside, ao ar livre
with a view, com vela vista
on the patio, no pátio

on the balcony, na varanda
no smoking, não fumante

where is...?, Onde é...?
the toilet, toilette/banheiro
men, homen/macho
women, mulher/fêmea
the bill, conta
a mistake (error), erro
Is service included?, A gorjeta esta
    incluída?
Do you accept credit cards?,
    Aceitam cartão de crédito?
Do you accept traveler's checks?,
    Aceitam cheque de viagem?
How much?, Quanto custa?
I did not order this., Não pedi isto.
this is , este é
(not) fresh, (não) fresco
not cooked, não cozido
burnt, queimado
too (much) , demais
cold, frio
hot, quente
fresh, fresco
rare, mal passado
overcooked, está cozinhado demais
delicious, delicioso
cheap/expensive, barato/caro
good/bad, bo/podre
less/more, menos/mais

without shellfish, sem mariscos

closed, fechado
open, aberto

monday, segunda-feira
tuesday, terça-feira
wednesday, quarta-feira
thursday, quinta-feira
friday, sexta-feira
saturday, sábado
sunday, domingo

January, Janeiro
February, Fevereiro
March, Março
April, Abril
May, Maio
June, Junho
July, Julho
August, Agosto
September, Septembro
October, Outubro
November, Novembro
December, Dezembro

I am a vegetarian., Sou vegetariano.
I am on a diet., Estou de regime.
I am allergic., Sou alérgico.
I am a diabetic., Sou diabético.
I am drunk., Estou inebriado.

I cannot eat..., Não posso comer...
without meat, sem carne
without pork, sem porco

Portuguese to English

à/à moda de, in the style of
abacate, avocado
abacaxi, pineapple
abóbora, pumpkin
abobrinha, zucchini
açafrão, saffron
acará/acarajé, fritters made from black beans and fried dried shrimp
acelga, Swiss chard
acepipes, hors d'ouevres/appetizers
acerola, a common type of cherry found in Brazil
acompanhamento, side dish/vegetables
açorda, a thick soup or a side dish. Bread is the main ingredient and there are many versions
açorda alentejana, *açorda* with garlic, poached eggs, coriander , olive oil
açorda de bacalhau, *açorda* with dried cod
açorda à moda Sesimbra, *açorda* with garlic, fish and coriander
açúcar, sugar
agri-doce, sweet and sour sauce
agrião, watercress
água, water
água gelada, ice water
água mineral, mineral water
água com gas, mineral water with carbonation
água sem gas, mineral water without carbonation
aguardente, brandy/aquavitae
aipim, a sweet tuber (root vegetable) .The skin is removed and it is eaten like a potato
aipo, celery
alcachofra, artichoke
alcaparra, caper
alcoólico, alcoholic
alecrim, rosemary
aletria, thin noodles (vermicelli). This also can refer to a dessert made with vermicelli, eggs and cream
alface, lettuce
alheira, garlic sausage
alheira à transmontana, garlic sausage served with fried potatoes, fried eggs and cabbage
alho, garlic
alhoporro, leek
à lista, a la carte
almoço, lunch
almôndega, fish or meat ball
amanteigado, buttered
amargo, bitter
amêijoa, small clam
amêijoas à Bulhão Pato, clams fried in olive oil with coriander and garlic, This dish is named after a Portuguese poet
amêijoas à espanhola, baked clams with onions, garlic, tomatoes, peppers and herbs
amêijoas ao natural, clams steamed with herbs (and served with lemon

juice and melted butter)

ameixa, plum

ameixa seca, prune

amêndoa, almond

amendoim, peanut

à moda de, in the style of

amora, blackberry

amor em pedaços, bars made with cookie dough and topped with
  almonds and merengue (means "love in pieces")

ananás, pineapple

anchova, anchovy

angu de arroz nordestino, corn flour cooked with coconut milk and rice
  flour. A specialty in northeast Brazil

angu goiano, porridge made from green corn cobs. A specialty in
  central Brazil

anho à moda do Minho, roast lamb and rice dish

aniz, anis

angu, cassava root or corn boiled in water and salt

ao, in the style of

ao natural, plain. Also refers to drinks served at room temperature

ao ponto, medium

aperitivo, aperitif

arenque, herring

arroz, rice

arroz à grega, rice with peas, carrots, peppers and small pieces of ham.
  A specialty in the Rio de Janeiro region

arroz árabe, fried rice with dried fruits and nuts

arroz à valenciana, rice with pork, chicken and seafood

arroz brasileiro/arroz simples, rice sautéed in garlic, onion and oil
  before boiling

arroz branco, plain rice

arroz com feijão, rice browned in onion, oil and garlic before boiling, and
  served with black beans on the side

arroz com guariroba, rice dish with *guariroba* (a bitter coconut)

arroz de Cabidela, risotto with giblets and chicken blood

arroz de carreteiro, risotto containing meat, tomatoes and onions.
  A specialty in south Brazil

arroz de côco, rice cooked in coconut milk

arroz de frango, baked chicken and rice

arroz de manteiga, rice cooked in water and butter

arroz de marisco, rice with seafood

arroz de pato no forno, duck cooked in rice with bacon and pork sausage

arroz doce, sweet rice pudding

arroz do povo, rice cooked with slices of meat, onion beans and garlic

arroz mineiro, rice cooked with carrots, potatoes and minced meat

arroz tropeiro, rice with salted and dried meat

aspargo, asparagus

aspide, aspic

assado, roast

assado, roast/roasted

assado nas brassas, broiled

atum, tuna

aveia, oats

avelã, hazelnut

aves, poultry
avezia, flounder
azeda, sorrel
azedo, sour
azeite, olive oil
azeite de dendê, orange palm oil (from the African palm which grows in northern Brazil
azeitona, olive
azeitona preta, black olive
azeitona recheada, stuffed olive
azeitona verde, green olive
azeitona verde de Elvas, green olive
babá de moça, egg yolks poached in coconut milk and syrup
bacalhau, cod. Usually it is dried and salted. It is said that the Brazilians and Portuguese have as many ways to prepare cod as there are days in the year.
bacalhau à Brás, cod fried with onions and potatoes topped with beaten eggs then baked
bacalhau à Gomes de Sá, cod fried with onions, garlic, boiled potatoes (and usually served with hard-boiled eggs). This dish is named after the owner of a restaurant in Porto, Portugal
bacalhau à portuguesa, cod between layers of potatoes and tomatoes and baked
bacalhau à provinciana, cod, potato and turnips au gratin
bacalhau à transmontana, cod braised with cured pork, garlic, parsley, tomatoes and wine
bacalhau à Zé do Pipo, cod with an egg sauce
bacalhau com leite de coco, cod poached in coconut milk
bacalhau com natas no forno, boiled cod baked with potatoes and cream
bacalhau de caldeirada, cod braised with tomatoes, onions, garlic, coriander and parsley
bacalhau cozido com todos, poached cod served with boiled cabbage, potatoes and eggs
bacalhau fresco à Portuguesa, fresh cod with rice and vegetables
bacalhau na brasa, barbecued dried cod
bacon, bacon
bagaço, "firewater" a spirit distilled from grape skins
batata, potato
batata assada, baked potato
batata doce, sweet potato
batata frita, French Fry
batata sotê, boiled parsley potatoes

ORDERING MEAT
well done – *bem passado*
medium – *médio*
rare – *mal passado*

batida, fresh fruit juice and *cachaça* (Brazilian brandy made from sugar cane)
baunilha, vanilla
bavaroise, egg white and cream dessert
bebida, drink/beverage
beijinhos de moça, candies made from egg yolks, grated cheese and coconut
bem casados, sugar cookies bound together with a filling (means "well married")
bem passado, well-done
berbigão, a kind of cockle
berinjela, eggplant

besugo, sea bream
betteraba, beet
bifana, a slice of pork tenderloin in a bread roll
bife, steak
bife a cavalo, beef topped with a fried egg
bife à cortador, beef fried in garlic-butter
bife à milanesa, breaded veal scallops
bife à portuguesa, steak with a mustard sauce and usually topped
   with a fried egg
bife de atum, tuna steak
bife de cebolada, steak with onions
bife de espadarte, swordfish steak fried with potatoes and onions
bife de javali, wild boar steak
bife de vaca, steak
bife de vaca com ovo a cavalo, steak with an egg on top
bife grelhado, grilled steak
bifinhos de porco, small slices of pork
bifinhos de vitela, veal served with Madeira wine
bifinhos na brasa, slices of barbecued beef
biscoito, cookie
biscoitos de maizena, cornstarch cookies
bobó, dried shrimp, onions, cassava root and coconut milk dish
boi, beef
bola de Berlim, donut (usually jelly-filled)
bolacha, cookie
bolacha de água e sal, cracker
bolinho de bacalhau, deep-fried cod ball
bolinho de queijo, deep-fried cheese ball
bolo, cake
bolo caseiro, home-made cake
bolo de carne, deep-fried ball of dough
   with a meat center/filling
bolo de chocolate, chocolate cake
bolo de nozes, walnut cake
bolo inglês, spongecake containing dried fruit
bolo podre, honey- and cinnamon-flavored cake
bolo rei, a Christmas ring cake
bomba de creme, cream puff
bombom de uva, grape surrounded by a sugar and egg mixture
borracho, young pigeon
borrego, lamb
branco, white
brande, brandy
brasa, charcoal-grilled
brigadeiros, a rich chocolate fudge-like dessert, usually in a ball shape
brioche, croissant
broa, dark bread with a hard crust from northern Portugal
brócolos, broccoli
bruto, extra-dry
cabeça, head
cabeça de pescada, fish head dish
cabidela, giblets
cabreiro, goat's cheese
cabrito, kid

cabrito assado, roast kid
cabrito-montês, roebuck
cabrito à ribatejana, kid marinated and roasted with herbs
caça, game
cacau, cocoa
caçador(a), simmered in wine with onions, carrots and herbs
cachola frita, fried pig's heart dish
cachorro quente, hot dog
cachucho, small sea bream
café, coffee
café da manhã, breakfast
café com leite, coffee with milk
café duplo, two espressos in one cup
café glacé, iced coffee
café instantâneo, instant coffee
cafezinho, strong coffee with sugar
caipirinha, lemon, sugar and *cachaça*
caju, cashew nut
calamar, squid
caldeirada, fish stew with tomatoes, onions, potatoes, wine and herbs
caldeirada à fragateira, fish and mussels in tomato and herbs
caldeirada à moda da Póvoa, sea bass, eel, cod and hake, simmered with tomatoes and olive oil
caldeirada de enguias, eel *caldeirada*
caldo, soup/broth
caldo de aves, poultry (usually chicken) soup
caldo verde, thick soup with cabbage, potatoes and smoked pork sausage
camarão (camarões), shrimp
camarão com côco, shrimp cooked in coconut milk
camarão frito, fried shrimp
camarão seco, dried shrimp
camarões empanados, shrimp fried in batter
camarões à Baiana, shrimp in a spicy tomato sauce
camarões à paulista, shrimp marinated in garlic, onion, lemon juice, vinegar and fried in oil
camarões grandes, jumbo shrimp
cambuquira, squash stewed with meat
canapé, small open-faced sandwich
canela, cinnamon
canja, rice and chicken stew
canja de galinha, chicken stew
canjica, sweet-corn and peanuts cooked in milk and served with fresh coconut milk (check)
capão, capon
caqui, persimmon
caracol (caracóis), snail. This also refers to a snail-shaped bun usually filled with currants
caranguejo, crab
carapau, similar to a sardine
carapau de escabeche, *carapau* fried and in a sauce of olive-oil, fried onions, garlic and vinegar
cardápio, menu
caril, curry
carmelizado, glazed

carne, meat
carne à jardineira, meat and vegetable stew
carne assado, roast meat
carne de carneiro, mutton
carne de porco, pork
carne de porco à alentejana, marinated pork fried with clams
carne de sol, meat which is salted and dried in the sun
carne de vaca, beef
carne de vinha, pickled pork dish
carne de vitela, veal
carneiro, mutton
carneiro guisado, mutton stewed with tomatoes, parsley,
    garlic and bay leaf
carne picada, minced meat
carne seca, dried meat
carnes frias, cold cuts
carta, flounder
carta de vinhos, wine list
caruru, spiced dish made from *quiabo* (okra) and stewed
    with dried shrimp
caruru do par, shrimp and okra dish
cuscuz à paulista, corn flour cooked with cabbage, peppers, tomatoes,
    eggs and chicken. A specialty from São Paulo
caseiro, home-made
casquinhas de siri, crab meat served in a shell
casquinho de caranguejo, baked crab meat
casquinho de lagosta, lobster prepared with butter, onion, milk
    and potatoes and served in its shell
castanha, chestnut
castanha de caju, cashew
castanhas do Pará, Brazil nuts
cataplana, steamed in a copper pan
catupiri, fresh fat cheese made from cow's milk
cavala, mackerel
ceia, dinner
cebola, onion
cebolada, fried onion (a garnish)
cenoura, carrot
centeio, pão de, rye bread
cereja, cherry
cerveja, beer
cerveja branca, lager
cerveja de pressão, draft beer
cerveja preta, dark, bitter beer
cevada, barley. This also refers to a popular coffee-like drink
chá, tea
chá com limão, tea with lemon
chá de limão, hot lemon tea
champanhe, champagne
chanfana de porco, pork casserole
chantilly, whipped cream
charlotte, cookies with cream and fruit
chávena, cup
cherne, a type of grouper

BE POLITE!

please – *por favor*

thank you – *obrigado (spoken
by a man)/obrigada (spoken by
a woman)*

gentleman – *senhor*

woman – *senhora*

miss – *menina*

I'm sorry. – *Desculpe.*

Excuse me. – *Com licença.*

chicória, chicory/endive
chimarrão, strong tea in southern Brazil. It's served hot
   without sugar from a pipe-like cup
chispalhada, pig's feet-based stew
chispe, pig's foot
choco, cuttlefish
choco com tinta, cuttlefish cooked in its own ink
chocolate, chocolate
chocolate quente, hot chocolate
chopp, draft beer
chouriça/chouriço, spicy smoked pork sausage (with paprika)
chuchu, summer squash
churrasco, barbecued meats and sausages grilled on skewers
churrasco à Gaúcha, grilled meats
churros, thin long fritters
cidra, cider
cimbalino, small espresso
cocada, coconut macaroon
coco, cononut
coco gelado, chilled cononut water
coco loco, coconut and chocolate dessert
codorniz, quail
coelho, rabbit
coelho a caçadora, rabbit and rice casserole
coelho assado, roast rabbit
coelho de escabeche, marinated rabbit
coentro, coriander
cogumelo, button mushroom
colorau, paprika
colher, spoon
com, with
com gás, carbonated
com gelo, with ice
comida, meal
comida congelada, frozen food
cominha, caraway seed
compota, stewed fruit
congro, conger eel
conquilhas, baby clams
conta, check (the bill)
copo, glass
coquetel de camarão, shrimp cocktail
coração, heart
coracãoes de alcachofa, artichoke hearts
cordeiro, lamb
corvina, croaker fish
costeleta, cutlet/chop (or is it costoleta?)
costeleta de porco, pork chop
costelinhas de carneiro, lamb chops
couve, cabbage
couve à mineira, green cabbage and bacon
couve branca, white cabbage
couve-de-Bruxelas, Brussels sprouts
couve-flor, cauliflower

SPECIAL NEEDS
allergic – *alérgico*
diabetic – *diabético*
diarrhea – *diarréia*
diet – *dieta*
dirty – *sujo*
disabled –
deficiente físico
doctor – *médico*
drunk – *bébedo*
emergency – *emergência*
food poisoning –
intoxicação alimentar
nausea – *naúsea*
non-alcoholic – *analcoólico*
non-smoker – *não-fumador*

couve galega, galician cabbage (somewhat bitter)
couve lombarda, savoy cabbage
couve portuguesa, cabbage which is similar to *couve galega*
couvert, cover charge
couve roxa, red cabbage
coxinha, pastry filled with chicken, meat, shrimp or cheese
cozido, cooked/boiled/boiled stew
cozido à brasileira, stew with many ingredients including meats,
    sausages, plantains, sweet potatoes and corn on the cob
cozido à portuguesa, stew of boiled sausages, potatoes, vegetables
    (usually carrots, turnips and cabbage) and meats
cozido em lume brando, simmered
cozidos, ovos, hard-boiled eggs
creme, cream
creme de abacate, sweet avocado cream dessert
creme de cogumelos, cream of mushroom soup
cremem de mariscos, cream of seafood soup
crepe, crepe
creme de leite, fresh cream
criação, livestock
cristalizada, candied
croquetes de camarões, shrimp croquettes
croissant, crescent roll
cru/crua, raw
crustáceo, crustacean
cubo de gelo, ice cube
curau, mashed sweet-corn cooked in coconut milk
damasco, apricot
descafeinado, decaffeinated
dióspiro, persimmon
dobrada/dobradinha, tripe
dobrada à moda do Porto, tripe and bean dish
doce, sweet/jam. This also refers to candy
doce de laranja, marmalade
doce de ovos, egg custard
dose, portion
dose para crianças, children's portion
dourada, dory (a saltwater fish)
dourado, browned
éclair, éclair
efo, pieces of grouper in a mixture of coconut milk and ground peanuts
eiró, eel
ementa, menu/set-priced menu
ementa fixa, fixed-priced menu
ementa turística, tourist menu (usually fixed-priced)
empada, small pie
empadinha, empanada (turnover filled with various ingredients)
empadão, large pie
empadão de batata, minced meat with mashed potato topping
    (shepherd's pie)
empanado, breaded
em sangue, rare
encharcada, dessert made of eggs and almonds
enchidos, assorted pork made into sausage

33

endívia, endive
enguia, eel
ensopado, stew
entradas, appetizers
entrecosto, sparerib
ervanço, chickpea
ervas, herbs
ervilha, pea

ervilhas reboçadas, buttered peas with bacon
escabeche, sauce of olive-oil, garlic, fried onions and vinegar
escalfado, poached
escalope, veal scallop (thin slices of veal)
escalope ao Madeira, veal scallop in Madeira wine
escalope de vitela, veal scallop (thin slices of veal)
escalope panado, breaded veal scallop
esfirra, pastry filled with spiced meat
espadarte, swordfish
espaguete, spaghetti
espaguete à bolognese, spaghetti in a tomato and meat sauce
espargo, asparagus
esparregado, creamy purée of assorted greens
especial da casa, specialty of the house
especiaria, spice
espetada, kebab
espeto, roasted on a spit
espinafre, spinach
espinafres gratinados, browned spinach with cheese sauce
espumante, sparkling
estragão, tarragon
estrelados, ovos, sunny side up eggs
estufada, stew
estufado, braised/stewed
esturjão, sturgeon
expresso, espresso
faca, knife
faisão, pheasant
farinha, flour
farinha de aveia, oatmeal
farofa, cassava-root meal browned and buttered
farófias, meringues floating in a cream sauce (means "floating island")
farturas, long, thin fritters
fatia, slice
fatias da China, baked egg yolks topped with syrup and cinnamon
    and served cold
fatias douradas, french toast
fatias recheadas, slices of bread with fried minced meat
favas, broad beans
febras de porco à alentejana, pieces of grilled pork fillet
feijão (feijões), bean
feijão à brasileira, meat and black bean dish
feijão branco, navy bean
feijão carrapato, green bean
feijão catarino, pink bean
feijão com peixe, black beans with fish. A specialty of the

Espírito Santo Region of Brazil

feijão encarnado, red bean

feijão frade, black-eyed bean

feijão guisado, bean dish stewed with bacon in tomato sauce

feijão-manteiga, beans cooked and browned in butter and parsley

feijão preto, black bean

feijão tropeiro, black bean dish (fried with meat which has been salted
and dried in the sun)

feijão verde, green bean

feijoada, black bean stew cooked with different meats and
served with rice on the side

fiambre, ham

fígado, liver

fígado de aves, chicken liver

figo, fig

figo seco, fried fig

filé, steak, pork, chicken or veal slices fried and served
with rice and beans

filé de peixe com molho de camarão, fish fillet with a shrimp sauce

filete, fillet

filhó, fritter

filhozes, sugar buns

fios de ovos, beaten egg yolk and sugar dessert

fofos de bacalhau, codfish balls

folhado, puff pastry

folhado de carne, meat in pastry

folhado de salsicha, sausage roll

forma, pão de, white bread

forno, baked

framboesa, raspberry

frango, chicken

frango à caipira, risotto made with chicken pieces.
A specialty in south Brazil

frango ao vinho, chicken breast in red wine sauce

frango assado, roast chicken

frango com catupiry, chicken browned in pork fat with
pieces of *catupiry* cheese

frango com creme de milho, chicken cooked with a corn-based cream

frango com farofa, chicken served with cassava root meal and mixed with
olives, giblets and hard-boiled eggs

frango com quiabo, pieces of chicken cooked in broth with chopped okra

frango na púcara, chicken casserole
flavored with port wine

frango no churrasco, barbecued chicken

frango no espeto, spit-roasted chicken

fresco, fresh

fressura de porco guisada, pork offal casserole

fricassé, casserole

frigideira, meat, seafood and/or vegetables topped with beaten eggs and
baked. This is the word for frying pan

frio, cold

fritada de carne, meat and sausages fried with eggs and cheese

fritada de peixe, deep-fried fish

frito, fried/fritter

fruta, fruit
fruta em calda, fruit in syrup
fruta da época, seasonal fruit
fruta do conde, mixed tropical fruit
fruta cristalizada, candied fruit
fubá, cornflour
fumado, smoked
funcho, fennel
fundo de alcachofra, artichoke bottom
fungo, strong pungent mushroom
galantina, meat in gelatine
galão, large coffee with a lot of milk (served in a tall glass)
galeto, cockerel cut in pieces, sprinkled with lemon and grilled.
A specialty from the south of Brazil
galeto na brasa, charcoal-broiled chicken
galinha, chicken
galinha corada, baked chicken
galinha de África, guinea fowl
galinhola, woodcock/snipe
gambas, shimp
ganso, goose
garçon, waiter
garçonete, waitress
garfo, fork
garoupa, large grouper
garrafa, bottle
garrafeira, aged red wine
garoto, small coffee with milk
gasoso, carbonated
gaspacho, purée of tomatoes, vinegar, onions, green peppers, garlic,   cucumbers and bread crumbs (chilled)
gelado, ice cream
geléia, jelly/jam
gelo, ice
gengibre, ginger
ginja, a sour cherry
goiaba, guava
goiabada, guava paste
gombo, okra
gordo, fat
gordura, fat
gorjeta, tip
grão, chickpeas
grão-de-bico, chickpeas
grão com bacalhau, chickpea and dried cod stew
gratinado, oven browned
grelhado, grilled
grelos, turnip greens
groselha, red currant
guaraná, a tropical fruit made into juice and soft drinks
guardanapo, napkin
guariroba, bitter coconut
guisado, stewed

TROPICAL FRUITS
banana – *banana*
coconut – *coco*
grapefruit – *toranja*
guava – *goiaba*
kiwi – *kiwi*
mango – *manga*
orange – *laranja*
passion fruit – *maracujá*
pineapple – *abacaxi*

hambúrguer, hamburger
hambúrguer no pão, hamburger in a roll
hortaliça, green vegetable
hortelã, mint
imperial, a glass of beer (about 1/4 liter)
incluído, included
inhame, yam
inhoque, potato dumplings (the Brazilian version of gnocchi)
iogurte, yoghurt
iscas, liver which is thinly sliced
iscas à portuguesa, thin slices of calf's liver marinated in garlic, wine and bay leaves (cooked in a shallow earthenware dish)
italiana, half of a strong espresso
jabuticaba, bing cherry
jacaré, small crocodile found in northern Brazil
jambu, a type of cress
jantar, dinner
jardineira, mixed vegetables
jarro, jug
javali, wild boar
lagosta, lobster
lagosta à americana, flaming lobster dish with Madeira wine, herbs, tomatoes and garlic
lagosta suada, lobster with tomatoes, garlic and onions in a port wine sauce
lagosta Thermidor, flaming lobster dish with white wine, herbs, spices and mustard
lagostim, prawn
lagostim-do-rio, fresh-water crayfish
lampreia, lamprey fish
lampreia de ovos, dessert (in the shape of a lamprey fish) made of eggs and sugar
lanche, snack
laranja, orange
lasanha, lasagne
lavagante, lobster
lebre, hare
legumes, vegetables
legumes variados, mixed vegetables
leitão, suckling pig
leitão à Bairrada, roasted suckling pig (coated with a spicy sauce)
leitão assado, roast suckling pig
leitão recheado, roasted stuffed (with a spicy mixture) suckling pig
leite, milk
leite-creme, custard dessert
lentilha, lentil
licor, liqueur
ligeira, a light snack (usually means a bite or two)
lima, lime
limão, lemon
limão verde, lime
limonada, lemon juice with sugar and water
língua, tongue
linguado, sole/flounder

> **IS THE TIP INCLUDED?**
> *A gorjeta esta incluída?*

37

linguado à meunière, sole (dipped in flour) sauteed in butter and served with lemon-juice and parsley

linguíça, pork sausage flavored with paprika

lista, list/menu

lista de preços, price list

lista dos vinhos, wine list

lombinho, pork loin

lombo, loin

lombo de vaca, sirloin

louro, bay leaf

lulas, squid

maçã, apple

maçã assada, baked apple

maçapão/massapão, marzipan/almond macaroon

macaxeira, cassava root

macedónia de frutas, fruit cocktail

Madeira, dry and sweet fortified wine

maduro, mature

maionese, mayonnaise

maionese de alho, garlic mayonnaise

malaguete, hot pepper

mal passado, rare

Malvasia, a sweet Madeira wine

mamão, papaya

mandioca, cassava root

manga, mango

manjar, a delicacy

manjar de coco, coconut pudding

manjericão, basil

manteiga, butter

manteiga queimada, a butter sauce used on fish dishes

mãozinhas de vitela guisadas, calves' feet dish

maracujá, passion fruit

maragarina, margarine

marinado, marinated

marinheira, a dish served with parsley, onions, wine and tomatoes

mariscada, Brazilian *bouillabaisse*

marisco, seafood

marmelada, quince jelly

marmelo, quince

massa, pastry/dough/pasta

mazagrin, iced coffee with lemon

medalhão, medallion

medalhão com arroz à piemontese, thick steak medallion wrapped in bacon and fried and served with rice with a creamy sauce

meia de leite, large white coffee

meia desfeita, dried cod fried with onions, vinegar and chickpeas and topped with garlic and hard-boiled eggs

meia dose, half portion

meia garrafa, half bottle

médio, medium

mel, honey

melancia, watermelon

melão, melon

melão com presunto, melon with cured ham
melão com vinho do Madeira, Madeira wine poured over melon
melão com vinho do Porto, port poured over melon
merenda, snack
merengue, meringue
merengue de morango, strawberry meringue
mero, red grouper
meunière, à, sauteed in butter and served with lemon-juice and parsley
mexidos, ovos, scrambled eggs
mexilhão, mussel
mexerica, tangerine
migas, slices of bread dampened with olive oil and flavored with garlic
mil-folhas, napoleon
milho doce, sweet-corn
mingau, porridge
Minho, do, a dish served in a port wine, brandy, blood and spice sauce
mioleira, brains
miolos, brains
miolos mexidos com ovos, fried lamb brains and scrambled eggs
misto, mixed
miúdos de galinha, chicken giblets
mocotós, stewed calves' feet dish
moleza, soup made with pig's blood
molho, sauce/gravy
molho ao Madeira, Madeira wine sauce
molho apimentado, hot sauce
molho bearnaise, béarnise sauce (hollandaise sauce (melted butter, egg
  yolks and lemon juice) with vinegar, tarragon, shallots and wine
molho béchamel, white sauce (usually butter, milk [and/or cream]
  and flour)
molho branco, white sauce
molho de camarão, sauce made from shrimp cooked in coconut milk,
flour and chili. Frequently found in dishes in the Bahia region of Brazil
molho de manteiga, butter and lemon sauce
molho à Espanhola, spicy garlic and onion sauce
molho holandês, sauce of melted butter, egg yolks and lemon juice
  (hollandaise sauce)
molho inglês, Worcherstershire sauce
molho mornay, cheese sauce
molho tártaro, tartare sauce
molho veloutée, sauce made from egg yolks and cream
molho verde, green sauce of parsley, olive-oil, vinegar, spinach and
  coriander leaves
moqueca de camarão, stew of shrimp in tomatoes, onions, cilantro,
  coconut milk and *dendê*
moqueca de peixe, fish dish with coconut milk, ginger and
  ground shrimp
morango, strawberry
morango silvestre, wild strawberry
morcela, blood sausage
mortadela, bologna
moscatel, muscatel wine
mostarda, mustard
mousse, mousse

mousse de chocolate, chocolate mousse

muçuã, small turtle

muito mal passado, rare

mumu de siri, crabs cooked with tomatoes, onions and other ingredients

nabiça, turnip greens

nabo, turnip

na cataplana, steamed in a copper pan

na brasa, charcoal-grilled

na frigideira, sautéed

não, no

não alcoôlico, non-alcoholic

napolitanas, cookies

nas brasas, braised

nata, cream

nata batida, whipped cream

natural, plain

nectarina, nectarine

nêspera, a small fruit similar to a plum

no churrasco, barbecued

no espeto, roasted on a spit

no forno, baked

noz, nut

noz muscada, nutmeg

óleo, oil

óleo de amendoim, peanut oil

ôlhos de sogra, prunes stuffed with coconut and rolled in sugar

omeleta/omelete, omelette

omeleta simples, plain omelette

orelha, ear

osso, bone

ostras, oysters

ouriço-do-mar, sea urchin

ovas, fish roe

ovo, egg

ovo cozido, hard-boiled egg

ovo escalfado, poached egg

ovo estrelado, sunny side up egg

ovo estrelado com fiambre, fried ham and egg

ovo quente, soft-boiled eggs

ovos mexidos, scrambled eggs

ovos moles, beaten egg yolks in syrup

ovos queimados, sweet egg dish

ovos verdes, eggs stuffed with hard-boiled yolks which are mixed with an onion, vinegar and olive-oil mixture

paca, meat, similar to pork, roasted with bacon, onion, pepper and garlic

paçoca, roasted carne del sol with cassava root and bananas. This can also refer to roasted peanuts with sweet cassava root

paio, spicy cured pork

palha de ovos, egg pastries

palmito, palm shoots. They look like short white sticks and are eaten alone or in salads

pamonhas, corn husks stuffed with a paste made of corn, coconut, sugar and spices

panado, breaded

LET'S EAT!
breakfast – *café-da-manhã*
lunch – *almoço*
supper – *jantar*
dinner – *ceia*

panqueca, pancake
pão, bread
pão branco, white bread
pão de centeio, rye bread
pão de forma, white bread
pão-de-ló, spongecake/angel food cake
pão de milho, corn bread
pão de queija, cheese bread
pão integral, wholewheat bread
pão ralado, breadcrumbs
pão torrado, toast
pãozinho, roll
papos de anjo, baked egg yolks topped with syrup
páprica, paprika
pargo, dentex (a fish)
parrilhada, grilled fish
passa, raisin
passa de uva, raisin
passado bem, well done
passado, mal, rare
pastéis, pastries
pastéis de bacalhau, dried cod fishcakes
pastéis de carne, puff pastry filled with meat
pastéis de queijo, cheese-filled fried dumpling
pasteis fritos, fried turnovers
pastel, pie
pastelão de Vila Velha, flour, milk, eggs and lard pudding.
  A specialty in south Brazil
pastel de bacalhau, deep-fried dried cod and mash potato dish
pastel de Belém, custard pie
pastel de nata, custard pie
pastel folhado, flaky pastry
pastel de massa tenra, pie filled with minced meat
pastel de Santa Clara, small tart with almond filling
pastel de Tentúgal, pastry with a filling of beaten eggs cooked in syrup
pastelinhos de bacalhau, dried cod fishcakes
pataniscas, fritters
paté, pâté
pato, duck
pato ao tucupi, roast duck braised with carrots in cassava-root juice
pato com laranja, duck à l'orange
pé de moleque, peanut brittle
pé de porco, pig's feet
peito, breast. *Peito de frango* is a chicken breast
peixe, fish
peixe à Mato Grosso, fish wrapped in banana leaves and roasted
peixe à moda capixaba, pieces of fish marinated with various spices
peixe espada, sword fish
peixe frito, fried fish. In northeast Brazil, this refers to fish marinated in
  lemon, sal, pepper and garlic, dipped in flour and fried in oil
peixe da horta, green beans deep-fried in batter
peixinhos da horta, green bean fritters
pepino, cucumber/pickle
pequeno almoço, breakfast (used only in Portugal)

pêra, pear
pêra abacate, avocado
pêra bela helena, pear in a chocolate sauce
perca, perch
percebe, similar to a barnacle
perdiz, partridge
perdiz na púcara, partridge casserole
perna, leg
perna de carneiro assada, roast leg of lamb
perna de carneiro entremeada, stuffed roast leg of lamb
pernil, ham
perninhas de rã, frogs' legs
pêro, a type of apple
peru, turkey
peru assado à Califórnia, roast turkey with fruit
peru à brasileiro, stuffed and roasted turkey
pescada, whiting
pescada cozido dom todos, whiting served with green beans and potatoes
pescadinhas de rabo na boca, dish of fried whitings (served with their
    tails in their mouths)
pêssego, peach
pêssego careca, nectarine
pevide, seed. This can also refer to salted pumpkin seeds
picadinho, chopped meat mixed with tomatoes, onions and peppers
picado de carne, minced meat
picante, spicy/hot/highly seasoned
pimenta, pepper
pimenta preta, black pepper
pimentão, sweet pepper
piemontesa, creamy sauce made from grated cheese, butter, mushroom
    and wine. Usually served over rice
pingo, small coffee with milk
pinhão, pine nut
pinhoada, candied pine nut kernel
pio nonos, spongecake with guava paste
piperate, pepper stew
pirarucú, a freshwater fish indigenous to Brazil
piri-piri, small hot peppers. This also refers to a seasoning made
    from hot peppers and olive oil
pitú, freshwater lobster
pitú con côco, freshwater lobster, marinated and cooked with pieces of
    coconut. A specialty of the Espírito Santo region of Brazil
polvo, octopus
pombo, pigeon
ponche, punch
ponta de espargo, asparagus tip
porção, portion
porco, pork
porco recheado, roast stuffed pork
posta, slice of meat or fish
prato, dish/plate
prato do dia, plate of the day
prato especial da casa, specialty of the house
prato principal, main course

preço, price
preço variado, price varies. Abbreviated as p.v.
prego, small steak (usually in a bread roll)
prego no pão, steak sandwich
prego no prato, steak served with a fried egg
pré-pagamento, pay in advance
presunto, cured ham
puchero de Paraná, beef cooked with garlic, tomatoes, peppers and
   onion. A specialty in south Brazil
pudim, pudding
pudim de bacalhau, dried cod loaf
pudim flan, caramel custard
pudim à portuguesa, custard flavored
   with brandy
puré, purée
puré de batata, mashed potatoes
queijada, dessert made of grated coconut and cheese, milk and egg yolks
queijinhos do céu, marzipan rolled in sugar
queijo, cheese
queijo cabreiro, goat cheese
queijo cardiga, goat and ewe's-milk cheese
queijo catupiri, cream cheese
queijo curado, white, mature, hard cheese
queijo da ilha, similar to cheddar and
   flavored with pepper. From the Azores
queijo da serra, a goat's cheese found in northeastern Portugal
queijo de cabra, goat's cheese
queijo de ovelha, sheep's cheese
queijo de Palmela, white, mild cheese
queijo Minas, cheese made of cow's milk. It is white, slightly salted
   and fat free
queijo Prato, mild, yellow cheese
queijo rabaçal, a goat's milk cheese
queijo requeijão, a type of cottage cheese
queijo São Jorge, similar to cheddar cheese
quente, hot
quente e frio, hot-fudge sundae
quiabo, okra
quibe, meat loaf dish from São Paulo
quibebe, pumpkin purée
quindim, egg and coconut dessert
rabada ensopada, oxtail stew
rabanada, french toast
rabanete, radish
raia, skate
ralado, grated
receita, recipe
recheado, stuffed
recheio, stuffing
recheio de carne, meat filling
refeição, meal
refeição ligeira, snack
refogado, onions fried in olive oil

refresco, juice
refrigerante, soda
regionais, regional
remoulade, mustard and herb dressing
repolho, cabbage
requeijão, curd cheese
reserva, high quality aged wine
ricota, similar to Italian ricotta cheese
rillete, potted pork
rins, kidneys
risol, deep-fried meat patties
robalo, sea bass
rodela, a round slice
rodízio de massas, pasta (of different sizes and shapes) in one dish. This
    is found on many menus in Rio de Janeiro
rojões, pork cubes
rolo de carne, meatloaf
rolos de couve lombarda, stuffed cabbage leaves
    (with sausage or minced meat inside)
romã, pomegranate
rosca, ring-shaped white bread
roupa velha, shredded beef in a tomato-based sauce (means "old clothes")
ruivo, red gurnard fish
safio, conger eel
sal, salt
salada, salad
salada de alface, green salad
salada de atum, tuna salad
salada de fruta, fruit salad
salada de macarrão, cold pasta salad
salada de ovos, egg salad
salada de palmito, salad made of palm shoots
salada mista, mixed salad
salada russa, cooked, diced vegetables and potatoes served in mayonnaise
    (Russian potato salad)
salgadinhos de bacalhau, cod mixed with mashed potatoes
    and deep fried
salgado, salty/salted
salmão, salmon
salmão fumado, smoked salmon
salmonete, mullet
salpicão, mixed salad which often contains slices of chicken. The salad
    dressing is usually creamy mayonnaise
salsa, parsley
salsicha, sausage
salsicha de coquetel, cocktail sausage
salsicha de peru, turkey sausage
salteado, sautéed
salva, sage
sande, sandwich
sanduíche, sandwich
santola, large crayfish
saquinho, bag. *Saquinho de chá* is a tea bag
sarda, mackerel

ON A DOOR	
open –	*aberto*
closed –	*fechado*
entrance –	*entrada*
exit –	*saída*
push –	*empurre*
pull –	*puxe*

44

sardinha, sardine
saudades, dessert made of sugar, tapioca and egg yolks
sauté, sautéed
sável, shad
seco, dry/dried
seleção, selection. *Seleção de queijos* is a selection of cheeses
sem gas, without carbonation
sem gelo, without ice
sêmola, semolina
sericá alentejano, cinnamon soufflé
serviço incluído, service included
siri, crab
siri recheado, crab shell stuffed with crabmeat, tomatoes, onions and
  peppers
sirva gelado, served chilled
sobremesa, dessert
solha, sole
sonho, a type of donut
sopa, soup
sopa à Alentejana, soup made using coriander, garlic browned in oil,
bread and eggs
sopa de agriões, watercress and potato soup
sopa de beterraba, beet soup
sopa de cebola gratinada, fresh onion soup
sopa de coentros, soup with bread, poached eggs, coriander leaves, garlic
  and olive oil
sopa de feijão, soup with carrots, kidney beans, rice and cabbage
sopa de feijão preto, black bean soup
sopa de hortaliça, fresh vegetable soup
sopa de hortelã, mint soup
sopa de macaxeira, soup made from the root *aipim*
sopa de milho verde, green corn cob soup
sopa de palmito, cream of hearts-of-palm soup
sopa de panela, egg-based dessert
sopa de pedra, thick vegetable soup
sopa de rabo de boi, oxtail soup
sopa de siri, creamy crab soup
sopa de tartaruga, turtle soup
sopa de tomate à alentejana, soup with onions, tomatoes and
  poached eggs
sopa do dia, soup of the day
sopa e cozido, meat stew
sopa juliana, shredded vegetable soup
sopa leão velloso, seafood chowder
sopa transmontana, soup with ham, bacon, vegetables and bread
sorvete, ice-cream
sorvete com àgua, sherbet
strogonoff à moda do Paraná, fillet browned in garlic and butter with a
  sauce of cream, tomato and mushroom. A specialty of south Brazil
suco, juice (usually fruit, sugar, ice and water in a blender)
suco de laranja, orange juice
supremo de frango, boned and breaded chicken breast
sururu, a type of cockle
suspiro, meringue (means "sigh")

tacacá, soup of dried shrimp and tapioca
tainha, grey mullet fish
tâmara, date
tangerina, tangerine
tarifas de consumo, price list
tartaruga, turtle
tarte, tart/quiche
taxa de serviço, service charge
tempero, seasoning
tempero de salada, salad dressing
tenro, tender
tigelada, eggs beaten with milk and cinnamon
tomar, soft fresh goat's cheese
tomate, tomato
tomilho, tender
toranja, grapefruit
tornedó, round cut of beef (tournedos)
torrada, toast
torrão de ovos, marzipan
torresmos, fried pork fat and skin
torta, pie/tart/patty
torta de Viana, roll filled with lemon curd
tosta, toasted sandwich
tosta mista, toasted ham and cheese sandwich
tortilha, omelet
tortilha de mariscos, omelet filled with shellfish
toucinho, bacon
toucinho do céu, marzipan pudding
toucinho fumado, bacon
tripas, tripe
tripas à moda do Porto, tripe cooked with assorted pork,
    chicken, vegetables and beans and served with rice
trouxas de ovos, sweetened egg yolks topped with syrup
trufa, truffle
truta, trout
turlu-furnu, baked eggplant, onions, potatoes and tomatoes
tutano, marrow
tutu à mineira/tutu mineiro, black beans mixed with cassava-root
uva, grape
uva passa, raisin
vaca, beef
vaca cozida, boiled beef
vaca estufada, beef stew
vagens, green beans
variado, assorted
vatapá, shrimp and fish puree which is flavored with coconut milk and
    usually served with a cashew and peanut sauce
veado, venison
vegitariano, vegetarian
velha, old, mature (as in liquor)
velhíssma, very old, mature liquor
vermute, vermouth
vieira, scallop
vinagre, vinegar

ON THE TABLE	
spoon –	*colher*
fork –	*garfo*
knife –	*faca*
napkin –	*guardanap*
glass –	*copo*
salt –	*sal*
pepper –	*pimenta*
menu –	*cardápio*
candle –	*vela*
plate –	*prato*

46

vinho, wine
vinho branco, white wine
vinho claro, unfortified wine
vinho da casa, house wine
vinho da Madeira, Madeira wine
vinho de mesa, table wine
vinho de Xerêz, sherry
vinho do Porto, port wine
vinho espumante, sparkling wine
vinho generoso, wine fortified with brandy
vinho moscatel, muscatel wine
vinho rosé, rosé wine
vinho spumoso, sparkling wine
vinho tinto, red wine
vinho verde, green wine made from unripened grapes. It is young, slightly sparkling and acidic. You drink it chilled
vitela, veal
viveiro de mariscos, seafood stew
xalota, green onion
xarope, cordial
xícara, cup
ximxim, stew
ximxim de galinha, chicken served with a sauce made of peanuts, ginger, sweet peppers, onions and ground shrimp. This is a specialty of the Bahia region of Brazil

---

WINE

red – *vinho tinto*
white – *vinho branco*
rose – *vinho rosé*
corkscrew – *saca-rolhas*

47

Spanish Pronunciation Guide

If you are looking for a comprehensive guide to speaking Spanish, this is not the the right place. What follows are simply a few tips for speaking Spanish and a very brief pronunciation guide.

It is always good to learn a few polite terms so that you can excuse yourself when you've stepped on the foot of an elderly lady or spilled your drink down the back of the gentleman in front of you. It's also just common courtesy to greet the people you meet in your hotel, in shops and restaurants in their own language.

The Spanish language is actually very straightforward. Unlike English, every letter is pronounced in Spanish, even the final vowels on words ending with *e*'s. The one major exception is the double *l* which is pronounced like a *y* (tortilla) in Central and most of South America, or *sh,* in Spain and some parts of South America.

The last syllable is stressed in words ending with a consonant except *n* and *s*.

The next to the last syllable is stressed in words ending with *n* and *s* and in words ending in a vowel.

If a word is an exception to the above rules, an accent appears over the vowel of the stressed syllable.

a like *ah*
b usually the same as in English, but sometimes like a *v*
c similar to the English *k*
c before *e* and *i*, similar to the English *s* or *th* (in Spain)
chthe same as in English
d similar to the English d, except at the end of a word or between vowels, like th
e like e in they
f the same as in English
g like g in gate
g before *e* and *i*, like the English j
h not pronounced in Spanish
i like the English e
j like a throaty h
k the same as in English (and in words of foreign origin)
l the same as in English
ll like a *y* in Central and most of South America, like an *sh* in Spain

and some of South America

m the same as English

n the same as English

ñ like a combination of *n* and *y* as in canyon

o like *oh*

p the same as English

q pronounced like a k

r pronounced like an *r* with the tip of the tongue against the ridge of the gums

rr a strong rolled r sound

s the same as English

t the same as English

u like the u in crude

v like the English *b*, except like the English *v* within a word

w the same as in English (and only found in words of foreign origin)

y the same as in English, except when alone like ee in meet. In Argentina and Uruguay like a combination of *j* and *z*

z like *th* in Spain and like *s* in all other Spanish-speaking countries

English to Spanish

This is a brief listing of some familiar English foods and food-related words that you may need in a restaurant setting. It is followed by a list of phrases that may come in handy.

anchovy, anchoa
appetizer, una tapa
apple, manzana
artichoke, alcachofa
ashtray, cenicero
asparagus, espárragos
avocado, aguacate
bacon, tocino/beicon
baked, al horno
banana, banana. Do not confuse this with *plátano*
bean, judía/frijole/habichuela
beef, carne de vaca/buey
beef steak, bistec/biftec
beer, cerveza
beverage, bebida
bill, la cuenta
bitter, amargo
boiled, hervido
bottle (half), media botella
bottle, botella
bowl, tazón
bread roll, panecillo/pancito
bread, pan
breakfast, desayuno
broiled, asado
broth, caldo
butter, mantequilla
cabbage, repollo/col
cake, una torta/un pastel
candle, vela
carrot, zanahoria
cereal, cereal
chair, silla
check, la cuenta
cheers, salud
cheese, queso
cherry, cereza
chicken soup, caldo de gallina/sopa de pollo

chicken, pollo
chop, chuleta
clam, almeja
cocktail, aperitivo/cóctel
cod, bacalao
coffee, café
coffee with hot water (to dilute), café con agua caliente
coffee with milk, café con leche
coffee (black), café negro
coffee (decaf), café descafeinado
coffee (small cup) with milk or cream, café cortado
cold, frío
condiment, condimento
corn, maíz
cottage cheese, requesón
cover charge, cubierto
cucumber, pepino
cup, taza
demitasse/black coffee, café solo
dessert, postre
dinner, cena/comida
dish (plate), plato
drink, bebida
duck, pato
egg, huevo
espresso, café exprés
fish, pescado
fish soup, sopa de pescado
fork, tenedor
fowl, gallina
french fries, patatas fritas
fresh, fresco
fried, frito
fruit, fruta
game, carne de caza
garlic, ajo
gin, ginebra
glass, vaso

glass with stem, copa
goat (baby), cabrito
grape, uva
grapefruit, pomelo/toronja
green bean, judías verde
grilled, a la parilla/plancha
ham (boiled), lacón
ham (cured), jamón
hamburger, hamburguesa
honey, miel
hors d'oeuvre, entremeses
hot, caliente
ice, hielo
ice cream, helado
iced coffee, café granizado
iced tea, té helado
ice (on the rocks), con hielo
ice water, agua helada
ketchup, salsa de tomate
knife, cuchillo
lamb, cordero
large, grande
lemon, limón
lettuce, lechuga
little (a little), poco
liver, hígado
lobster, langosta
loin, lomo
lunch, almuerzo
mango, mango
marinated, escabeche
match, fósforo/cerilla
mayonnaise (with), alli olli
meat, carne
medium (cooked), regular/un
  poquito crudo
melon, melón
menu, la carta/el menú
milk, leche
mineral water, agua mineral
mineral water (sparkling), agua
  mineral gaseoso or con gas
mineral water (without carbonation), agua mineral sin gas
mixed, mixta
mushroom, seta/champiñon
mussel, mejillón

mustard, mostaza
napkin, servilleta
noodles, tallarines
octopus, pulpo
oil, aceite
olive oil, aceite de oliva
omelette, tortilla
on the rocks (with ice), con hielo
onion, cebolla
orange, naranja
orange juice, jugo de naranja
overdone, demasiado hecha
oyster, ostra
partridge, perdiz
pastry, pastel
peach, melocotón
pear, pera
pea, guisante
pepper (spice), pimienta
pepper (vegetable), pimiento
perch, mero
pineapple, piña
plantain, plátano
plate (dish), plato
please, por favor
plum, ciruela
poached, hervido
pork, cerdo/puerco
potato, patata
poultry, aves
prawn, gamba/langostinos
quail, codorniz
rabbit, conejo
rare, cruda/poco hecha
raspberry, frambuesa
raspberry, frambuesa
receipt, recibo
rice, arroz
rice pudding, arroz con leche
roasted, asado
salad, ensalada
salt, sal
salty, salado
sandwich, sandwich, bocadillo
  or torta
sauce, salsa
saucer, platillo

sautéed, salteado
scallop, vieira
scrambled, revuelto
seafood, mariscos
seasoning, condimento
sherry, jerez
shrimp, camarón/gamba
small, pequeño
smoked, ahumado
snail, caracol
sole, lenguado
soup, sopa/caldo
sparkling (wine), espumoso
specialty, specialidad
spinach, espinaca
spoon, cuchara
squid, calamar
steak, filete
steamed, cocido al vapor
stewed, estofado
strawberry, fresa
sugar, azúcar
sugar substitute, sacarina
supper, cena
sweet, dulce
table, mesa
tea, té
tea with lemon, té con limón
tea with milk, té con leche
teaspoon, cucharilla
tenderloin, solomillo/filete
thank you, gracias
tip, propina
toasted, tostado
tomato, tomate
trout, trucha
tumbler (glass), vaso
tuna, atún/bonito
turkey, pavo
utensil, utensilio
veal, ternera
vegetable, legumbre/verdura
vegetarian, vegeteriano
venison, venado
vinegar, vinagre
vodka, vodka
waiter, camarero/señor
waitress, camarera/señora
   or señorita

Helpful Phrases

please, por favor (*por fah-bor*)
thank you, gracias (*grah-thee-ahs*)
you are welcome, de nada (*deh-nah-da*)
yes, sí (*see*)
no, no (*no*)
good day, buenos días (*bway-nohs dee-ahs*)
good afternoon/evening, buenas tardes (*bway-nahs tar-days*)
good night, buenas noches (*bway-nahs noh-chays*)
hello, hola (*oh-la*)
goodbye, adiós (*ah-dee-ohs*)
I am sorry, lo siento (*low see-en-toh*)
do you speak English?, ¿habla usted inglés? (*ah-blah oo-stehd een-glays*)
excuse me, perdóneme (*pehr-doh-nay-may*)
I don't understand, no comprendo (*no kohm-prehn-doh*)
help, ayuda (*a-yoo-dah*)
where is...?, ¿donde esta...? (*dohn-day ay-stah*)
where are...?, ¿donde están...? (*dohn-day ay-stahn*)
the toilets, los servicios (*lohs sehr-bee-thee-ohs*)
men, hombres (*ohm-brays*)
women, mujeres (*moo-heh-rays*)
Mr., señor (*sayn-yor*)
Mrs., señora (*sayn-yoh-rah*)
Miss, señorita (*sayn-yoh-ree-tah*)
waiter, camarero (*kah-mah-ray-roh*)
waitress, camarera (*kah-mah-ray-rah*)
what, qué (*kay*)
when, cuándo (*kwahn-do*)

how, como (*koh-mo*)

who, quién (*kee-ehn*)

why, por qué (*por kay*)

this, esto (*ay-stoh*)

I'd like…, quiero… (*kee-ehr-oh*)

the bill, la cuenta (*la kwayn-tah*)

a room, una habitación (*oo-nah ah-bee-tah-thee-ohn*)

a ticket, el billete (*bee yay-tay*)

a table, una mesa (*oo-nah may-sah*)

I want to reserve a table, quiero reservar una mesa (*kee-ehr-oh ray-sehr-bar oo-nah may-sah*)

for one, para uno (1) (*oo-no*), dos (2) (*dohs*), tres (3) (*trays*), cuatro (4) (*kwah-troh*), cinco (5) (*theen-koh*), seis (6) (*says*), siete (7) (*see-eh-tay*), ocho (8) (*oh-choh*), nueve (9) (*n'weh-bay*), diez (10) (*dee-ayth*)

now, ahora (*ah-oh-ra*)

today, hoy (*oy*)

tomorrow, mañana (*mahn-yah-nah*)

outside, a fuera (*ah-fwaira*)

inside, dentro (*dentro*)

no smoking, no fumadores (*no foo-mah-doh-rays*)

a mistake (error), un error (*oon her-ror*)

is service included?, ¿está el servicio incluido? (*ay-stah ehl sehr-bee-thee-oh een-kloo-ee-doh*) or ¿está incluida la propina? (*ay-stah een-kloo-ee-dah la proh-pee-nah*)

credit card, tarjeta de crédito (*tar-hay-tah day kray-dee-toh*)

what is this?, ¿qué es esto? (*kay ays ay-stoh*)

I did not order this, no ordené esto (*no or-day-nay ay-stoh*)

this is, esto es (*ay-stoh ays*)

cold, frío(a) (*free-oh*)

undercooked, crudo (*kroo-doh*)

overcooked, muy hecho (*moo-ee ay-choh*)

delicious, delicioso (*day-lee-thee-oh-soh*)

cheap/expensive, barato(a)/caro(a) (*bah-rah-toh/kah-roh*)

good/bad, bueno(a)/malo(a) (*bway-no/mah-loh*)

less/more, menos/más (*may nohs/mahs*)

the same, el mismo (*ehl mees-moh*)

another, otro (*oh-troh*)

I am drunk, soy borracho (*soy boh-rah-choh*)

I am a vegetarian, soy vegetariano(a) (*soy bay-hay-tah-ree-ah-noh*)

I am diabetic, soy diabético(a) (*soy dee-ah-bay-tee-koh*)

without meat, sin carne (*seen car-nay*)

without seafood, sin mariscos (*seen mah-ree-skohs*)

without pork, sin cerdo (*seen thehr-doh*)

without sugar, sin azúcar (*seen ath-oo-car*)

open, abierto (*ah-bee-yehr-toh*)

closed, cerrado (*thehr-rah-doh*)

Monday, lunes (*loo-nays*)

Tuesday, martes (*mar-tays*)

Wednesday, miércoles (*mee-ehr-koh-lays*)

Thursday, jueves (*hway-bays*)

Friday, viernes (*bee-ehr-nays*)

Saturday, sábado (*sah-bah-doh*)

Sunday, domingo (*doh-meen-goh*)

a caballo, steak topped with eggs

a punto, medium done

a su gusto, your own way

abadejo, fresh cod

aberezada, with dressing

aberezo de la mesa, condiments

abichón, sand smelt

abocado, semi-sweet table wine

abodado, marinated

acedera, sorrel

acedia, baby sole

aceite, oil

aceite de girosol, sunflower oil

aceite de oliva, olive oil

aceite de palma, palm oil

aceite de soja, soy-bean oil

aceituna, olive

aceituna negra, black olive

aceituna verde, green olive

aceitunas aliñadas, olives with salad dressing

aceitunas rellenas, stuffed olives

acelga, beet greens/beets/Swiss chard

acerola, wild cherry

achicoria, chicory/endive

achiote, annatto-seed paste

aderezo (de mesa), condiments

adobadas, pickled

adobo, marinated prior to cooking. This can also refer to marinated fried fish

adobos de carne, meat marinades

agridulce, sweet and sour

agua, water

aguacate, avocado

agua de azahar, orange- or lemon-blossom water

agua de coca, coconut water

agua de grifo, tap water

agua de panela, drink made from water and sugar

agua de sel, seltzer or soda water

agua destilada, distilled water

A caballo means ∴ on horseback.

Aceite, the word for oil, is derived from Aceituna, the word for olive.

We drink bottled water as often as we can, for the taste as much as for purity.

agua dulce, boiled water with brown sugar

agua fresca, sweet, water-based beverage flavored with fruit

agua helada, ice water

agua mineral, mineral water

agua mineral con gas, mineral water (sparkling)

agua mineral gaseoso, mineral water (sparkling)

agua mineral sin gas, mineral water (without carbonation)

agua potable, drinking water

agua purificado/agua puro, purified water

aguardiente, strong liqueur made from the pressings of grape skins. In
Latin America, sugar-cane or corn-based liquor

aguja, needlefish/sparkling beverage

agujas, en, on skewers

ahumado, smoked

ahumados variados, smoked fish

ajada, garlic and oil sauce

ajedrea, savory

ajetes, garlic shoots

ají, chili, red pepper

ají de gallina, shredded chicken in a cream and pepper sauce

ajiaceite, garlic oil/garlic mayonnaise

ajiaco bogotano, thick potato soup (frequently with chicken)

ajilla, garlic sauce

ajillo, cooked in garlic and oil

ajillo moruno, Moorish casserole of bread, almonds, chopped beef or
liver, garlic and seasonings

ajo, al, contains whole garlic cloves

ajo, garlic

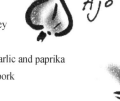

ajo arriero, with garlic, paprika and parsley

ajo blanco, cold almond and garlic soup

ajocabañil, meat prepared with vinegar, garlic and paprika

ajo de Mataero, dish of bacon, liver and pork

ajonjolí, sesame seed

ajopollo, chicken with garlic and almond sauce

al, a la, with/in the style of

aladroc, anchovies

alajú, cake with honey and almonds

alas, wings

albacora, swordfish

albahaca, basil

Albacora.

albardado, in a batter

albaricoque, apricot

albariño, al, in a white-wine sauce

albariño, white wine

albóndigas, meatballs/fishballs

Albondigas are often served as appetizers.

albufera, sauce with red pepper, almonds and cream

alcachofa, artichoke

alcachofas a la andaluza, artichokes with bacon and ham

alcaparra, caper

alcapurias, ground plantains with fish or meat fried in batter

alcaravea, caraway seed

alcohólica, alcoholic beverage

alfajores, small round cakes

algar-robina, *pisco* and carob syrup

alicantina, a la, with green peppers, artichokes and seafood

aliñada, marinated or seasoned or with salad dressing

aliño, dressing

alioli/ali oli/all-i-oli, garlic mayonnaise/garlic purée

allada, garlic and oil sauce

ali-pebre/all-i-pebre, garlic, oil and paprika sauce

almadrote, sauce with garlic, cheese and eggplant

almejas, clams

almejas a la buena mujer, clams in a wine and parsley sauce

almejas a la marinera, clams in a white sauce

almejas al natural/almejas naturales, live clams

almendrada, cooked with almonds

almendras, almonds

A la buena mujer means of the good woman.

almendras garrapiñadas, sugar-coated toasted almonds

almendras saladas, salted almonds

almendras tostadas, toasted almonds

almíbar, syrup

almojábanas, syrup-coated buns/corn muffins

almuerzo, lunch

aloque, red wine (made from a mixture of white and red grapes)

alpargata, sweet biscuit

alubias, kidney beans/broad beans/fava beans

Alubias blancas are white beans, rojas are red, rosadas, pink.

amanida, salad with fish and meat

amargo, bitter

amarilla, en, sauce with saffron and onions

amarillos (en dulce), ripe (yellow) plantains fried in a red wine, sugar and
   cinnamon sauce

amontillado, medium-dry sherry, older than *jerez fino,* aged at least eight
   years in wood

anacardos, cashews

anafre, bean paste smothered with melted cheese

ananás, pineapples

ancas de rana, frog legs

ancho, dried *poblano* pepper

anchoas, anchovies

anchoas a la barquera, anchovies with capers

andalucía, dry sherry and orange juice

andaluza, a la, with red peppers, tomatoes and garlic

añejo, aged

Ancas de rana

angélica, liquor similar to yellow Chartreuse

angelote, angelfish

anguila, eel

angula, baby eel

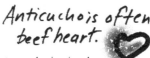

anguila

anís, anise/anise-flavored liquor

anisado, anise-flavored soda

anís seco, anise-flavored beverage

añojo, veal

anona, custard apple

anticucho, beef kebabs

Anticucho is often beef heart.

antojito, *tortilla* sandwich filled with beef, tomatoes and onions/snack

aperitivo, cocktail/aperitif

api, drink made from corn and cinnamon

apio, celery

arandano, cranberry

arencas, salted sardines

arenque, herring

arenque en escabeche, pickled herring

Armañac

arepa, corn-meal pancake or muffin

armañac, a type of brandy made from *aguardiente*

aromáticas, herbal teas

arroces, rice dishes

arrope, honey syrup

arròs, rice dish/soup with rice. *Arròs en cassola* is a dish of rice with
   assorted seafood from *Costa Brava*. *Arròs negre* is a squid and rice dish
   from *Catalonia*

arroz, rice

arroz a la banda, fish and rice with saffron

arroz a la catalana, rice with peppers and sausage

arroz a la Cubana, rice with tomato sauce, fried egg and banana

Arroz a la Cubana is sometimes made with banana instead of Tomato.

arroz a la emperatriz, rice with apricots, raisins, truffles, milk and Contreau

arroz a la española, rice with chicken livers, pork and tomatoes

arroz a la mexicana, a blend of tomatoes, rice and onions

arroz a la valenciana, rice with chicken, vegetables and shellfish

arroz a la vasca, rice with chicken giblets

arroz al canario, rice with ham and bananas

arroz al caldo, consommé with rice

arroz blanco, boiled, steamed rice

arroz brut, dry soup (see *sopas secas*) of rice and meats

arroz caldoso, rice soup

arroz con cacao, chocolate-flavored rice pudding

arroz con coco y titi, rice with coconut and shrimp

arroz con costra, rice (*paella*) with meatballs

Love this.

arroz con dulce, sweet rice pudding

arroz con habichuelas, rice and beans

arroz con leche, rice pudding

arroz con mariscos, rice with seafood

arroz con pollo, rice and chicken

arroz en caldero, rice with red peppers and seafood

arroz empedrat, rice with beans and tomatoes

arroz escarlata, rice with shrimp and tomatoes

arroz marinera, rice with assorted seafood

arroz moro, rice with spicy meat

arroz negro, rice made black by cooking in squid ink

arroz primavera, rice with vegetables

arvejas, peas

asadillo, roasted, skinned peppers with garlic

asado, roasted/roasted meats

asado de tira, spareribs

asador, grill room, rotisserie

asadurilla, lamb's liver stew

Asopao is Puerto Rico's most popular dish.

asopao, a thick stew made with rice and with meat or seafood

asturias, sharp-flavored cheese

ata, whipped cream

atole, oat-based beverage

atún, tuna

auyama, a fruit similar to pumpkin

avellana, hazelnuts

avena, oats. Can also refer to oatmeal

aves, poultry

atun.

azafrán, saffron

azahar, orange blossom

azúcada, sugared

azúcar, sugar

azúcar de acre, maple syrup

azúcar demerara, granulated brown sugar

azúcar enpolvo/azúcar glace, powdered sugar

azúcar moreno, brown sugar

babarrúa de naranja, frozen orange custard

bacalao/balcallao, salt cod

bacalao a la catalana, cod with ham, parsley, garlic and almonds

bacalao al ajo arriero, cod with parsley, garlic and peppers

bacalao a la riojana, cod and sauce with paprika and peppers

bacalao a la vizcaína, cod with ham, peppers, tomato sauce and potatoes

bacalao pil-pil, cod casserole with garlic and oil

bacalitos (fritos), fried cod fritters

bacon, bacon

baho, tomato and beef stew

bajoques farcides, meat and rice stuffed in red peppers

baleadada, *tortilla* filled with cheese, beans and eggs

banda de almendra, almond-and-marmalade puff pastry

bandarillo/banderillo, small skewer with ham, cheese or pickle

bandeja, de, tray of (as in tray of cheeses)

bandeja paisa, main dish. In Colombia this is a dish with ground beef,
   sausage, salt pork, beans, rice, avocado and fried egg.
   This dish is also called *plato montañero*

barbacoa, barbecued

barbo, barbel (a fresh-water fish)

barcoretta, tuna

barquillos, small cookies

barra, bar (as in a chocolate bar)

Barra de Pan is a loaf of Bread.

bartolillos, deep-fried pastry filled with custard

batata, sweet potato

batida/batido, milk shake

baveresa de coco, cold coconut dessert

Batata blanca is sweet potato with pink skin and yellow flesh.

bayas, berries

bebidas, beverages

bebidas alcohólicas, alcoholic beverages

bebidas refrescantes, soft drinks

becada, woodcock

beicon, bacon

berberecho, tiny clams found in Cantabria

berenjena, eggplant/aubergine

berenjena de Almagro, pickled eggplant

berenjena rebozada, battered and fried sliced eggplant

berenjenas a la mallorquina, eggplants with garlic mayonnaise

berraza, parsnip

berros, watercress

bertón, stuffed cabbage

berza, cabbage

besugo, sea bream/porgy

besugo a madrileña, baked bream with lemon and oil

besugo asado con piriñaca, bream baked with red peppers

besugo mechado, bream stuffed with bacon and ham

beterragas, sweet potatoes

bicarbonato de sosa, baking soda

bien cocido, well-done

bien hecho, well-done

bien-me-sabe coco, cake with coconut-cream topping

bien pasado, well-done

bife, steak

bife a lo pobre, large steak with fried potatoes and onions, served with two
   fried eggs on top

bife de lomo, T-bone steak served without the bone

biftec, beef steak

biftec de ternera/bistek de ternera, veal steak

biftec encebollado, steak with fried onions

biftek salteado al jerez, fried steak with sherry

bis/bisso, chub (mackerel)

bistek, beef steak

bizcocho, spongecake dessert

bizcochos borrachos, spongecake soaked in liquor (usually rum)
   and/or syrup

bizcotela, cookie

blanco y negro, iced milk, coffee and cinnamon

blando, soft

blanquillos, eggs

bocadillo, snack/sandwich usually with ham and cheese

bocadillos de monja (nun's mouthful), cake with egg, sugar and almonds

bocas, small appetizers served with alcoholic beverages

bodega, wine or sherry cellar

bogovante/bogavante, lobster

*No matter what
language
you say parsnip
in, it doesn't
sound good to us*

*Bien me sabe
means I know it
does me good.*

*Bistek –
Bien Cocido*

Bogovante

boletos, cepe/porcini mushrooms

bolillos, sandwich bread rolls

bolitas, cheese balls

bollito, bread roll/bun

bollo, bread roll/bun/breakfast roll baked with sugar

bollo de panizo, scone made of corn meal

bollo escocés, scone

bollo preñado, roll filled with meat

bollos de maíz, deep-fried corn puffs

bomba, meatball with chili sauce

bomba helada, baked Alaska

bombón, bonbon

boniato, similar, but not related, to a yam. Sometimes called a
Cuban sweet potato

bonito, tuna

Bonito are small tuna.

boquerones, anchovies

boquitas, small appetizers such as olives, peanuts or crackers

bori-bori, chicken soup with corn-meal balls

Boquitas means little mouths

borona, corn meal

borra, cod, spinach and potato soup

borracho, grey gurnard (seafood)

borrachos, cakes soaked in wine or syrup

botella, bottle

*Bo·tay·yah
May·dee·ah*

botella media, half bottle

botellín, small bottle of beer

bover, snail

brandada de bacalao, creamy cod purée

brasa, barbecued/grilled

braseado/a, braised

brazo de gitano, spongecake roll with custard filling

Brazo de gitano means gypsy arm.

breca, a type of sea bream

brécol, broccoli

brevas, deep-fried doughnuts with custard filling. In Latin America, this
refers to figs

bróccolis/bróculi, broccoli

brochetas, en, on skewers

broquil, broccoli

brotes, bean sprouts

brut, extremely dry wine

budín, pudding/custard

buey, beef

Not the budin found in creole countries which is blood sausage and is called Butifarra in Latin America.

buey de mar, large-clawed crab

buey estofado, beef stew with potatoes, sausage and wine

buñuelo, fried pastry/doughnut

buñuelo de bacalao, fried pastry with dried, salted cod

buñuelo de cuaresma rellenos, fried pastry with chocolate and cream

buñuelo de San Isidro, fried dessert pastry with sesame seeds and anise

buñuelo de viento, dessert of fried doughnuts with syrup

bunyettes, doughnuts

burgos, fresh, creamy white cheese

burrito, stuffed *tortilla*

búsano, whelk (seafood)

buseca, spicy oxtail soup. A specialty in Uruguay

butifarra, spiced sausage made of pork and/or veal. In Latin America, spicy blood sausage

buvangos rellenos, stuffed zucchini

caballa, mackerel

cabello de ángel, stewed sweet pumpkin or squash

cabeza de cerdo, brawn

cabeza de ternera, seasoned veal loaf/calf's head

cabra, goat. This can also refer to a spider crab in Catalonia

Cabeza de Cerdo is a fish but the name means Pig's head.

cabracho, scorpion fish

cabrales, a creamy blue cheese

cabrillo, comber (seafood)

cabrito, goat (kid)

cabrito asado roasted kid

cacao, cocoa

cacahuetes, peanuts

cacereña, black olive

cacerola, casserole

cachelada, potato and sausage stew

cachelos, diced, boiled potato dish

cachito, croissant

café, coffee

café americano, black coffee (diluted)

café con agua caliente, coffee with hot water (to dilute)

café con hielo, iced coffee

café con leche coffee with milk

café cortado, small cup of coffee with a small amount of milk or cream

café de olla, coffee with cinnamon and sugar

café descafeinado, decaffeinated coffee

café doble, large cup of coffee

café exprés, espresso

café grande, large cup of coffee

café granizado, iced coffee

café guayoyo, large cup of mild, black coffee

café irlandés, Irish coffee

Cafe Irlandés

café marrón, a large cup of strong coffee with a small amount of milk

café marroncito, small cup of strong coffee with a small amount of milk

café negrito, small cup of strong black coffee

café negro, black coffee

café perfumado, coffee with milk

café perico, coffee with liquor (usually brandy)

café solo, demitasse/black coffee

cafetería, self-service cafeteria

café tinto, black coffee

café vienés, black coffee and whipped cream

caguama, turtle

cailón, shark

caimito, star-shaped apple

you may want to make sure you're not eating an endangered species.

Caguama.

calabacín (or calabacita), zucchini

calabaza, pumpkin

calamares, squid

calamares a la romana, fried squid

calamares en su tinta, squid cooked in its own ink

calamares fritos, deep-fried squid

calamaritos, baby squid

calcots, spring onions

calda/caldo, hot

caldeirada, stew

calamares

caldera de dátiles de mar, seafood stew

caldereta, stew

caldereta asturiana, seafood stew

caldereta de cordero a la pastora, lamb and vegetable stew

caldereta de gallega, vegetable stew

caldereta de ternera, potted veal roast

caldero, cauldron

caldillo, clear fish soup

caldillo de congrio, conger-eel soup with potatoes and tomatoes

caldillo de perro, hake soup

caldo/calda, hot

caldo, broth/consommé

caldo de, soup

caldo de gallina, chicken soup

caldo de pescado, fish soup

caldo de res, beef stock and vegetable soup

caldo gallego, meat and vegetable soup (frequently ham and cabbage)

caldo guanche, soup with potatoes, tomatoes, onions, and zucchini

caldo verde, cabbage-based broth with potato and greens

caliente, hot. Often refers to a dish with a hot chili sauce

callampas, mushrooms

callos, tripe

callos a la catalana, tripe stew with wine and pine nuts

callos a la madrileña, tripe stew with peppers, sausage, ham and tomatoes

camarera, waitress

camarero, waiter

camarones, shrimp

camarones a la plancha, shrimp marinated and then grilled

camarones del rio, freshwater crayfish

camote, sweet potato

caña, mug of draft beer/alcoholic beverage from Paraguay made from sugar cane and similar to rum

caña de dulce, sugar cane

caña de vaca, marrow bone

cañadilla/cañailla, snail

canas, pastry cones filled with custard or cream

canela, cinnamon

canelones, cannelloni

canelones a la barcelonesa, ham and chicken-liver stuffed cannelloni

cangrejo (de mar), crab

cangrejo (de río), crayfish (river crab)

canilla, snack

canitas, pastry cones filled with custard or cream

cantarela, chanterelle mushroom

canutillos, custard-filled pastry horns topped
with cinnamon and powdered sugar

capirotada, meat dish in an almond sauce

capitán, *pisco* and vermouth

capitón, grey mullet

caqui, persimmon

carabineros, large shrimp

caracoles, snails. *Caracoles de carne* are meat-filled buns

carajillo, coffee with brandy

carajillo de ron, coffee with rum

carajillo de vodka, coffee with vodka

callampas.

cantarella.

Carojillo can also be served with Anisette.

64

carajitos, hazelnut macaroons

carambola, starfruit

caramelo, caramel

caraotas, beans

carbón, any charcoal-grilled filling

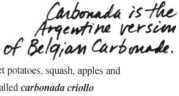

Carbonada is the Argentine version of Belgian Carbonade.

carbonada, beef stew, usually with rice, sweet potatoes, squash, apples and
   peaches (baked in a pumpkin shell); also called *carbonada criollo*

carbonada de buey, beef cooked in beer

carbonero, coalfish (cod)

cardamomo, cardamom

cardo, cardoon

cargol, snail

cargol.

cari, curry

carimañolas, turnover filled with cheese or meat

carne, meat

carne a la parilla, grilled steak

carne alambres, meat on a skewer

carne asada, grilled meat/barbecued beef

carne asada a la tampiqueña, beef steak with guacamole and beans

carne asada al horno, roast meat

carne de buey, beef

carne de caza, game

carne de cerdo, pork

carne de chancho, pork

carne de lidia, very tough beef

carne de mebrillo, quince jelly

carne de res, beef

carne de res con chile colorado, beef in red chile

carne de vaca, beef

carne en salsa, meat in tomato sauce

carne guisada, sauce with stewed beef

carne mechada, a beef roast served with onions, ham and spices

carne molida, ground beef

carne para asar, beef roast

carne picada, ground meat

carnero, mutton

carnero verde, mutton dish with parsley and mint

carnitas, barbecued pork

carpa, carp

carquinyolis, almond biscuit

carrillada, pig cheek

carpa.

carro de queso, cheese platter

carta, la, menu

carta de vinos, wine list

cártamo, safflower

casa, de la, of the house, could mean *specialty* or *homemade*

casadiellas, dessert turnovers

casados, fish, meat or chicken with rice, beans and vegetables

cáscara, rind/zest/peel/shell

casero, homemade

casi crudo, very rare

castañas, chestnuts

castellana, bread and garlic soup

castoñola, sea perch

catalana, a la, cooked in a tomato sauce

causa a la limeña, potato pureé with shrimp salad. A specialty from Peru

cava, sparkling wine

caza, game

cazadora, a la, with mushrooms, onions and herbs

cazón, dogfish/shark

a la cazadora.

cazón en adobo, shark marinated in vinegar, paprika, cumin and oregano;
    floured and deep-fried

cazuela, stew/casseroled. This also refers to a Puerto Rican pumpkin-
    and-coconut pudding

cazuela de ave, casserole with beans, corn, rice, pumpkin, carrots and spices.
    A specialty of Chile

cazuela de cordero, lamb stew with vegetables

cazuela de chichas, meat casserole

cazuelita, small casserole

cebada, barley

cebiche, see *ceviche*

cebolla, onion

cebollada, onion soup

cebolletas, scallions/chives

cebollinos, chives

cebrero, a creamy blue cheese

cecina, beef jerky/strip steak

cena, dinner/supper

cenicero, ashtray

centeno, rye bread

centollo, spider crab

centollo relleno, spider crab cooked in its shell

Cazuela is actually the name of the carthenware dish in which it is cooked.

cepa, wine grape

cerdo, pork

cereales, cereals

cerezas, cherries

cerveza, beer

cerveza de barril/cerveza de presión, draft beer

cerveza dorada, light (in color, not necessarily in calories) beer

cerveza extranjera, imported beer

cerveza negra, dark beer

cervecería, bar

césar/ensalada césar, Caesar salad

cesta de frutas, selection of fruit

cesta de frutas

ceviche, raw seafood marinated in lemon and lime juice;
frequently served as an appetizer

chabacano, apricot

chacina, ground sausage

chabacano.

chacoli, Basque white wine

chairo, lamb broth with *chuños* and vegetables. A Bolivian specialty

chajá, spongecake, cream and jam dessert

chalote, chalotas, shallots

chalupa, deep-fried *tortilla* with many fillings

champaña/champán, champagne

champiñon, mushroom

chancetes, deep-fried small fish similar to whitebait

chancho, pork

chanfaina, pig stew with rice and blood sausage

chanfaina castellana, rice and sheep's-liver stew

changurro, Basque dish of seasoned crabmeat

chanquetes, deep-fried small fish similar to whitebait

chapin, trunkfish (found in Puerto Rico)

chato, glass of red wine

chauchas, green beans

chayote, pear-shaped vegetable similar to squash

cherna, grouper

Chalupa, which actually means boat, is named for the boat shape of the finished tortilla.

choto.

chica, alcoholic beverage of fermented grapes and juice

chica de jora, alcoholic beverage made from corn.
The non-alcoholic version is *chica morada*

chica de manzana, apple brandy

chicha, an alcoholic beverage made from corn

chicharos, peas

chicharro, mackerel

chicharos.

chicharrones, pork fat/fried pork rinds/fried pork skin

chicharrones de pollo, crispy fried chicken pieces

chichicuilotes, small sparrows boiled live, served stuffed with avocado

chico zapote, the tropical fruit sapodilla found in Mexico

chifa, Chinese food

chilaquiles, pieces of fried *tortillas* with onions, red peppers, cheese and sour cream

chilcano, *pisco* and ginger ale

chile, chili pepper. Sweet to horribly hot and all shapes and colors! The Scoville scale ranks the fire power of a chili pepper. The hottest is a *haba ñero* with a measure of 100,000 to 300,000 units. In comparison, a *jalapeño* has a rank of 2500-5000 units

chile poblano, green pepper

chiles en nogada, green peppers stuffed with whipped cream and nuts

chiles rellenos, stuffed peppers

chili, chili

chilindrón, refers to the use of red peppers and tomatoes in a dish. For example, *pollo chilindrón* is a dish of chicken with red peppers

chillo, red snapper

chiltepe, a chili of medium heat with a somewhat nutty flavor

chimichanga, deep-fried *tortilla* stuffed with beef, beans and chilies

chile.

chimichurri, barbecue sauce of tomatoes, garlic, onions

china, a sweet orange

chinola, passion fruit

chipas, bread made of corn flour, cheese and eggs

chipi chipi, clam soup

chipirón, small squid

chipotle, dark chili sauce/a smoked *jalapeño* pepper

chiquito, glass of red wine

chirimoyas, custard apple

chirivias, parsnips

chirmol, hot sauce made of onions, tomatoes and mint

chistorra, a narrow sausage with paprika

chivito, steak sandwich

chivito al plato, steak topped with a fried egg and served with potato salad, a green salad and french fries

chivo, goat, kid

choclo, pastel de, a corn casserole filled with a variety of meats and vegetables. This can also refer to corn on the cob

chocolate, chocolate

chocolate caliente, hot chocolate.

chocolate caliente.

    Chocolate a la española is a thick hot chocolate drink

chocolate churros y porras, extremely popular fried pastry. *Churros* are loops and *porras* are sticks of deep-fried batter and are often eaten at breakfast or bedtime with a cup of hot chocolate

chocolate con leche, hot chocolate milk

chocolate santafereño, hot chocolate and cheese

chocolatina, chocolate bar/candy bar

chocos, large squid/cuttlefish

cholga, giant mussels

chongos, cheese in a sweet syrup

chop, beer (usually draft beer)

chopa, a type of sea bream

chopitos, cuttlefish

choricero, chili

choripán, sausage baked in dough

choritos, small mussels

chorizo, cured sausage seasoned with paprika and garlic, almost always pork sausage. In Mexico, the sausage is usually made from fresh ground pork

chorizo de olla, sausage stew

choros, mussels

choto, baby goat. *Choto ajillo* is kid in a garlic casserole

chuchitos, meat and sauce in dough and wrapped in a corn husk

chuchuco, barley, meat and peppercorn soup

chucrut, sauerkraut

chufa, tiger nut

chufle, an alcoholic beverage from Bolivia made with *singani*, lemon juice and soda

chuleta, cutlet/chop

chuleta de cerdo a la asturiana, pork chop with apples in cider sauce

chuleta de gamo, venison

chuletita/chuletilla, small cutlet/small chop

chuletón, rib beef chop/large chop

chumbera/chumbo, prickly pear

chuños, freeze-dried potatoes from Bolivia and Peru (frequently mixed with meat, eggs or fish)

chupe de camarones, shrimp stew. *Chupe de mariscos* is seafood stew

chupete, sucker/lollipop

churisco, baked sausage

churrasco, grilled steak (usually a thin slice)

churros, loops of deep-fried batter often eaten with a cup of hot chocolate

cidra, squash/squash boiled in sugar

cidracayote de verano, summer squash

Chocolate is native to South America. Hot chocolate and chocolate drinks are ubiquitous in Latin America.

chumberas.

cierva, deer

cigala, prawn

cigalas cocidas, boiled prawns (sometimes lobster)

cigarra de mer, (clawless) lobster

cilantro, cilantro/coriander. This herb is used heavily in Mexico

cincho, hard cheese made from sheep's milk

ciruela, plum

ciruelas pasas/ciruelas secas, prunes

civet de liebre, marinated rabbit

clara, beverage made from a mixture of beer and lemonade

clara de huevo, egg white

clarete, light red wine/rosé wine

claro, light (in color)

clavo, clove

clementina, mandarin orange

clérico, wine and fruit juice

clima, al, at room temperature

coca, pie

coca amb pinxes, sardine pie

coca mallorquina, similar to a pizza

cocadas/cocados, coconut cakes

cocarois, similar to a pizza and topped with raisins and pine nuts

cochifrito, milk-fed lamb stew

cochifrito de cordero, highly seasoned lamb stew

cochinillo, suckling pig

cochinillo asado, roasted suckling pig

cochinita, chopped pork dish

cocido, cooked, boiled, simmered. Can also refer to stew

cocido al vapor, steamed

cochinello.

cocido castellano, thick stew with sausage, chickpeas, chicken, bacon, potatoes and other vegetables

cocido con leche, *maté* with milk

cocido envuelto, baked in parchment

cocido madrileño, (Madrid stew) stew made from meat, vegetables and chickpeas

cocina casera, home cooking

coco, coconut

coco loco, coconut-flavored alcoholic beverage from Mexico

cocoa, chocolate

cocochas, pieces of hake gills. See *kokoxas*

cocos, coconut cakes

cocos frios, chilled coconuts, tops chopped off, drunk with a straw. A specialty in Puerto Rico and the Dominican Republic

cóctel, cocktail

cóctel campechana marinera, oyster and shrimp cocktail

cóctel de camarón/cóctel de gamba, shrimp cocktail

cóctel de mariscos, seafood cocktail

codillo de cerdo, pig's feet

Cocos frios.

codoñate, quince, chestnut and honey cake

codoñate de nueces, walnut cake

codorniz (codornices), quail

codorniz al nido, quail in a "nest" of fried potatoes

codorniz en zurrón, quail in green peppers

cogollo de palmito, hearts of palm

cohombro, cucumber

Cohombro.

col, cabbage

col de Bruselas, Brussels sprout

cola, tail/oxtail

cola de mono, coffee, rum, milk and *pisco*. In Chile, this is *aguardiente*, coffee, sugar, milk, cinnamon and egg yolk. Similar to eggnog

colecillas de Bruselas, the Latin America expression for Brussels sprouts

coles, cabbage leaves

coliflor, cauliflower

coliflor con bechamel, cauliflower and cheese

collejas, corn salad

colmenilla, morel mushrooms

Cola de Mono means Monkey Tail.

comedor, dining room. You get a basic, inexpensive meal here. These eating establishments have become harder to find

comida, lunch/meal

comida corrida, is a fixed-price menu in Mexico and *comida corriente* is a fixed-priced menu in Central America

comino, cumin (used in Mexican chili powders)

compota, compote/stewed fruit

Completo.

completo, hot dog

con, with. Often, this is abbreviated as *c/*

con hielo, beverage served "on the rocks"

coñac, brandy/cognac

concentrado, concentrate. *Concentrado de tomate* is tomato paste

concha, conch

conchas finas, large scallops/Venus clam

conchas peregrinas, scallops

conchitas, the Peruvian word for scallops

condimentos, condiments/seasonings

conejo, rabbit

conejo del monte, wild rabbit

confitura, jam

congrio, conger eel

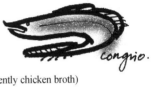

congrio.

conserva, pickled

consomé/consumado, clear soup (frequently chicken broth)

consomé a la reina, consommé with egg

consomé de chivo, goat soup

contra de ternera, veal stew

contrafilete de ternera, veal fillet

copa, glass

copa de helado, assorted ice creams served in a glass

copa nuria, egg whipped and served with jam

copetin, in Uruguay, any alcoholic beverage served with appetizers

copitas, sherry glass

coques/coquetes, flat bread, frequently used for pizza dough

coquinas, clams

coquito, holiday coconut eggnog with rum. A Puerto Rican specialty

corazón, heart/core. This is also the Puerto Rican word for a custard apple

corazón de alcachofa, artichoke heart

corazón de palma, hearts of palm

corazonada, hearts stewed in sauce

cordero, lamb

cordero al chilindrón, lamb with red peppers

cordero lechal asado, roast lamb

Cordero.

cordero mamón, suckling lamb

cordero recental, spring lamb

cortadillo, small pancake with lemon

cortado, coffee with a dash of milk

corto, glass of draft beer

corto.

corvina, white sea bass

corzo, deer

cosecha, vintage. *Cosechero* is the latest vintage of red wine

costada, flank

costellada, grilled lamb chops

costilla, chop/spareribs

costilla de cerdo con poco carne, spareribs

costra, crust

costrada, slice of cake or pastry

costrada navarra, thick soup topped with a bread crust

cranc verd, shore crab

crema, cream, mousse, or purée (soup). Can refer to sour cream in Mexico

crema batida, whipped cream

crema catalana, crème caramel

cremada, dessert made from sugar, milk and eggs

crema de arroz, creamy rice pudding

crema de cacao, chocolate liquor

crema de café, coffee liquor

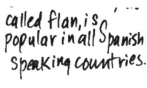
called flan, is popular in all Spanish speaking countries.

crema de maranja, curaçao, an orange-flavored cordial

crema de menta, crème de menthe

crema de San José, chilled custard

cremadina, custard filling

crema española, milk, eggs and fruit-jelly dessert

crema nieve, frothy egg-yolk, sugar, rum or wine beverage

cremas, sweet liquors

cremat, coffee with rum and brandy

cremat, cooked to golden brown

crepa/crep/crepe, crêpe. *Crepe imperial* is a crêpe suzette

criadillas, testicles/sweetbreads

criadillas de la tierra, truffles

Thanks, but No thanks.

crianza, wine aged in wood barrels

criolla, island cuisine which blends European, African, Taino and Arawak
Indian foods

That's Creole to us.

criolla, a la, with green peppers, tomatoes and spices

crocante, ice cream with chopped nuts

croquetas, fish, meat or vegetable croquettes. This can also refer to breaded
and deep-fried pieces of chicken, pork or beef, a specialty of Paraguay

cru de peix, fish stew which contains raw or slightly cooked fish

crudo, raw

cuajada, cream-based dessert with honey

cuarto, roast/joint

cubalibre, rum and coca-cola

cubana, a la, with eggs and fried bananas

Cuba Libre.

cubano, sandwich made of ham, chicken and/or pork, Swiss cheese, mustard
and pickles

cubata, liquor mixed with a soft drink

cubierto, cover charge

cubito de hielo, ice cube

cubra libre, rum and coca-cola. Sometimes this is gin and coca cola

cucaracha, *tequila* and coffee-flavored alcoholic beverage

cuchara, spoon

cuchifrito, a stew of pork innards
found in the Dominican Republic and Puerto Rico

cuchillo, knife

cuello, neck

cuenta, la, check/bill

cuerpo, de, full-bodied alcoholic beverage

cuitlacoche, a type of mushroom from Latin America

culantro, cilantro/coriander

curanto, A Chilean dish of meat (often suckling pig), vegetables
and seafood

curí, grilled guinea pig. A Colombian dish

cusuco, armadillo

cuy, grilled guinea pig. A Colombian dish

damasco, apricot

dátil, date

dátiles de mar, shellfish

de, of

delicias, small spongecake

delicias de queso, breaded and deep-fried cheese

dentón, dentex (a type of bream)

desayuno, breakfast

descafeinado, decaffeinated

despojos, innards (offal)

destornillador, "screwdriver": vodka and orange juice

diablo, al, spicy tomato sauce

día, del, "of the day"

diente de ajo, clove of garlic

doble, a large glass of beer

donastiarra, a la, charcoal grilled

dorada, sea bream/dolphin

duelos y quebrantos, scrambled eggs, ham and sausage

dulce, sweet/sweet wine

dulce de batata, thick slices of sweet potatoes. A specialty in Argentina

dulce de leche, milk simmered with vanilla and sugar and
served over toast or *flan*

dulce de membrillo, quince preserve

dulce de naranja, marmalade

duquesa, a type of fish or vegetable pie

durazno, peach

eglefino, haddock

ejotes, pole beans

elección, your choice

elotes, corn on the cob

emborrachada, marinated (means "drunk")

embuchado, stuffed with meat

embutido, fresh sausage

embutido de la tierra, local sausage

empanada (empanadas/os), turnover filled with various ingredients

empanada asturiana, turnover filled with *chorizo*

empanada de gallega, turnover filled with *chorizo*,
   chicken, ham, peppers and onions

empanada de horno, dough filled with ground meat/ravioli

empanada de lomo, pork and pepper turnover

empanada de pascua, lamb turnover

empanada de vieiras, scallop turnover

empanada salteña, ground meat with pepper, hot sauce, chicken,
   diced potatoes, olives and raisins wrapped in dough, then baked.

empanada santiaguesa, fish turnover or pie

empanadilla, small fish or meat patty.

Empanizada means breaded

emparador/emperador, swordfish

emparedado, hot sandwich

empedrada, salt cod and bean salad

encebollada, in an onion sauce/steak smothered in onions

enchilada, cheese-, chicken- or meat-filled *tortilla* topped with sauce.
   Enchiladas and *tacos* are both made of *tortillas* rolled around fillings.
   The difference is that an *enchilada* is baked with sauce over it and a
   taco is served with the sauce on the side

enchilada Oaxaqueña, Oaxaca, Mexico-style *enchilada* with sliced
   chiles poblanos, sour cream, grated cheese and sauce

enchilada roja, sausage-filled *tortilla*

enchilada suiza, stuffed corn *tortilla* topped with *tomatillo* sauce

enchilada verde, meat- or poultry-filled *tortilla* dipped in
   green tomato sauce

encurtido, pickle

endibia/endivia, chickory/endive

endrinas, blueberries

enebro, juniper berry

eneldo, dill

encurtido
de eneldo.

ensaimada, breakfast sweet roll. A Mallorcan specialty

ensalada, salad/rice salad

ensalada a la almoraina, salad with cumin and tomato dressing

ensalada a la catalana, cod and white-bean salad

ensalada común, green salad

ensalada de frutas, fruit salad

ensalada de habas, cooked bean salad

ensalada del tiempo, seasonal salad

ensalada de pepinos, cucumber salad

ensalada de piparrada, Basque tomato, cucumber and pepper salad

ensalada de pulpo, octopus salad.

ensalada de San Isidro, tuna, onion, tomato and lettuce salad

ensalada ilustrada, mixed salad

ensalada koshkera, Basque fish and lobster salad

ensalada mixta, mixed salad

ensalada simple, green salad

ensalada valenciana, salad with lettuce, potatoes and oranges

ensalada verde, green salad

ensaladilla rusa, Russian salad (cold potatoes and vegetables in mayonnaise)

entrada, appetizer

entrantes, starters/entrées

entrecot, entrecôt steak/filet mignon

entremés,entremeses, appetizers

entremeses variados, assorted *hors d'oeuvres*

epazote, tea made from an aromatic herb

erizo de mar, sea urchin. In Chile, *erizos* is a dish of raw sea urchins with pepper, salt, oil, onion and parsley. Frequently the sea urchin has a small crab attached to it. Eaten live!

escabeche, pickled/marinated. In Peru, this is a cooked, then chilled fish appetizer served with onions and peppers. In Mexico, this usually is fried fish or shellfish served in a spicy sauce. In the Dominican Republic and Puerto Rico, this refers to frying and then pickling fish, served hot or cold

escaldums, fried poultry in an onion and tomato sauce

arengue en escabeche is pickled herring.

escalfado, poached

escalibada, cod and vegetable salad

escalibada/escalivada, eggplant salad

escaloña, shallot

escalopa, boneless slice of meat

escalope de ternera, veal scallop

escalopines madrileños, veal with tomato sauce

escarcho, red gurnard, a type of fish

escarola, chickory/endive

escocés, scotch

escorpena/escorpión, scorpion

escudella, meat stew

espada/espaldilla, swordfish

espadin, sprat/whitebait

espaguetis italiana, spaghetti

espalda, shoulder

escocés con hielo.

esparragados, scrambled eggs and wild asparagus

espárrago, asparagus

espárragos amargueros, wild asparagus

espárragos calientes, asparagus with béchamel sauce

espárragos dos salsas, asparagus with mayonnaise and vinaigrette

espárragos trigueros, wild asparagus

especialidad, special

especialidad de la casa, house specialty/chef's specialty

especialidad de la región, regional specialty

especias, spices

espeto, cooked on a spit

espina, fish bone

espinaca, spinach

espinazo, ribs

espinas.

espuma de chocolate, chocolate mousse

espuma de jamón, ham mousse

espuma de mar, angel food cake with whipped cream.
   A specialty of Uruguay

espumoso, sparkling wine or beverage

esqueixada, red pepper, tomato and cod salad

estacíon, in season

estilo de, in the style of

estofado, stewed/braised.
   Estofados means stews

Estofado & fabada are favorite meals of ours.

estofado de vaca, garlic beef stew

estornino, mackerel (chub)

estragón, tarragon

faba/fave, a type of bean sometimes grown between rows of olive trees.
   Fabes/Faves (the plural of *faba/fave*) are dried for use in
   winter and eaten fresh in summer. Large and flat,
   they can be brown, beige or green.

fabada asturiana, pork, beans, sausage and bacon stew. The traditional
   version of this dish includes all cuts of pork, including feet and ears

fabes a la Catalana, stew with beans and black pudding

fabes a la granja, white-bean dish

fabricacion casera, homemade

faisán, pheasant

faisán a las uvas, pheasant and grapes cooked in port

faisán al modo de Alcántara, pheasant with port and truffles

faisán de Alcantara, pheasant in Madeira wine sauce

fajitas, really a "Tex-Mex" dish of grilled strips of meat or shrimp served on a sizzling plate and eaten with *tortillas*

faves.

falda rellena, stuffed flank

faramallas, sweet fritter

farinato, a sausage made from pork, flour and lard, generally eaten with fried eggs

farro, vegetable soup with barley

faves, see *faba/fave* above

fesol, dried bean

fiambre, any type of cold meat. In Guatemala, meat, fish and cheese salad

fiambre de bonito, tuna

fiambre de paleta, ham made of shoulder

fideos, noodles

fideua, noodle *paella*/baked noodle dish

filete, fillet (fish or steak). *Filete migñón* is filet mignon

filete de lenguado, fillet of sole

filete de lomo, tenderloin

filete de res, beef steak

filloas, filled crêpes

fino, pale, dry sherry

flamenca, a la, with sausage, green peppers, tomatoes, onions and peas

flamenquines, ham and/or cheese rolled into bread and then fried

flan, caramel-custard dessert

flan de café, coffee-flavored caramel custard

flaó/flaón, cheesecake

flauta, filled and deep-fried *tortilla* topped with sauce

flauta means flute.

flor de calabaza, pumpkin flower

flores, flower-shaped fritter

fonda, inn (frequently serving food)

fondo de alcachofas, artichoke heart

frambuesa, raspberry

francesa, a la, in a white sauce/sautéed in butter

fresas, strawberries

fresas de bosque, wild strawberries

fresco, chilled/fresh. In Central America, this refers to fruit juice

fresón, large strawberry

fricadelas, meat patties

fricandó, fried beef or veal

fricasé, a stewed chicken dish from Puerto Rico and the Dominican Republic (can also contain stewed goat or rabbit)

fricassé, pork cooked in a spicy sauce and served with potatoes and corn. A Bolivian specialty

frijoles, beans (kidney or red beans)

frijoles negros, black beans

frijoles refritos, (refried beans) beans mashed and fried

frío/fría, cold

fritada, fried pieces of meat

fritanga al modo alicante, tuna, fried peppers and garlic

frite, lamb fried with paprika. A specialty in the Spanish region of Extremadura

fritillas, rolls (frequently *fritillas al moro*, pork chunks wrapped in bacon and served on a toothpick)

frito, fried. This can also refer to a dish of fried offal and vegetables

frito de patata, deep-fried potato

fritos con jamón, fried eggs and ham

fritos de la casa, fried appetizers

fritura, fry. *Frituras*, fried bread

fritura (mixta) de pescado, fried mixed fish

frivolidades, assorted pastries

frixuelos, pancakes with honey

fruta, fruit

fruta de Aragón, chocolate-coated fruit

fruta escarchada, candied fruit (crystallized fruit)

frutas

frutas de mar, seafood

frutillas, strawberries. This word is used in Latin America

fuego de leña, al, charcoil broiled

fuerte, extremely spicy

fundido, fondue

gachas, porridge

fuerte can also mean rich. Literally it means strong.

gachas manchegas, sweet porridge

gallega, a la, with oil and paprika

galletas, crackers/cookies/biscuits/bread rolls

galletas de nata, sandwich cookies

gallina, chicken (hen)

gallina a la cairatraca, chicken stew

gallina.

gallina de guinea, guinea hen

gallina en pepitoria, chicken stew with almonds and/or peppers

gallineta, Norway haddock

gallo, rooster

gallo, flatfish

gallo en chica, rooster in El Salvador

gallo pinto, the national breakfast of Costa Rica.
Mixed cooked beans and rice.
Also found in Nicaragua

gallos, *tortilla* filled with meat and sauce

galludo, small shark

galupe, grey mullet

gambas, shrimp/prawns

gallo.

gallo pinto means painted rooster.

gambas a la americana, shrimp with garlic and brandy

gambas al ajillo, shrimp sizzled in oil and garlic

gambas a la plancha, grilled shrimp (in the shell)

gambas al pil-pil, shrimp with oil, garlic and hot peppers.
Served on toothpicks, this is a popular *tapa*

gambas con gardinas, battered, deep-fried shrimp

gambas con mayonesa, shrimp cocktail

gambas en garbardina, shrimp cooked in batter

gambas grandes, prawns

gandinga, spicy kidneys, hearts and livers

gandules, pigeon peas

ganso, goose

ganso

garbanzos, chickpeas

garbanzos a la catalana, chickpeas with sausage and tomatoes

garbanzos con espinacas, chickpea, spinach and garlic stew

garbure navarro, pork, vegetable
and sausage soup

garobo, iguana

garrapiñadas, glazed

gaseado, glazed

You can put garobo on the list with curl and cusoco.

gaseoso, drink with carbonation. This can also refer to carbonated lemonade

gâteau basque, filled sweet pastry

gazpacho (andaluz), purée of tomatoes,
vinegar, onions, green peppers, garlic,
cucumbers and bread crumbs (chilled)

gazpacho blanco, creamy, white *gazpacho* with almonds

gazpacho extremeño, white *gazpacho*

gazpacho malagueño, white *gazpacho* with grapes

gazpacho manchego, pâté of mixed game or
  stew of game, meat or poultry and vegetables
  and thickened with unleavened bread

gazpachuelo, soup with potatoes, mayonnaise, fish and vinegar

gelatina, gelatin

gelat, sorbet

jello- you just can't get away from it.

germen de trigo, ground duram wheat

ginebra, gin

girasol, sunflower

gitanilla, a la, with garlic

glorias, small sweet pastry

gol, alcoholic beverage from Chile made of milk, butter and sugar

gordal, large green olive

gorditas, small, thick *tortillas* filled with chopped meat, cheese, beans and
  vegetables, fried, and served with lettuce and chili sauce on top

gordo, fat/fatty

gracias, thank you

gorditas - deliciosas!!

granada, pomegranate

granadina, pomegranate syrup mixed with wine or brandy. This also refers
  to an eggplant and cured-ham loaf. This can also refer to an almond
  cookie

grande, large

granizado, fruit sorbet/crushed ice drink with fruit syrup or
  sweetened coffee

granos de maíz, sweet corn

gran reserva, wine of an exceptional vintage, aged for a long period of time

granvas, sparkling wine

gratén/gratín/gratinado, au gratin

greixera, casserole

greixonera de brossat, cheesecake made from cottage cheese

grelos, turnips/greens

grenadina, grenadine (pomegranate syrup)

grillado, boneless (for example, *pollo grillado* is boneless chicken)

grosella, currant

grosella espinosa, gooseberry

grosella negra, blackberry

grosella roja, red currant

grosella negra.

guacamole, avocado purée. In Mexico, a dip of mashed avocado, tomato,
  onion, cilantro and chilies

guanabana, custard apple

guandú, pigeon peas (beans)

guarapo, potent alcoholic beverage made from sugar cane

guarnición, garnish

guasacaca, relish of tomatoes, lime juice, onions and avocado

guayaba, guava. *Pasta de guayaba* is guava paste

guayoyo, large cup of mild, black coffee. Found in Venezuela

guinda, a sour black cherry

guindada, cherry brandy

guindilla, small, hot pepper/hot pepper sauce

guineo, Puerto Rican word for banana

guineitos verdes en escabeche, pickled green plantains. A Puerto Rican dish

guirlache, almond-and-anise candy similar to toffee

guisado, casserole/stew with cooked dish

guisantes, peas

guisantes a la española, peas with cured ham

guisat de cigrons, stewed chickpeas

guiso, stew/soup

guisantes.

guiso de maíz, thick corn stew. A Costa Rican dish

guiso de trigo, turnip soup

gusanos de maguey, fried white grubs. A dish found in parts of Mexico

gusto, a su, your own way

habañero, watch out! The hottest of all peppers

habas, beans. *Habas con jamón* is a casserole of ham and beans

habas a la andaluz, beans with cumin and artichoke

habas a la catalana, faba beans with sausages and meat

habichuela, bean

habichuela (verde), green bean

hallacas, meat and any number of ingredients and spices stuffed in dough
then wrapped in banana leaves and boiled in water

hamburguesa, hamburger

harina, flour

harina de maíz, corn meal

hecho, bien, well-done

hecho, muy, well-done

hecho, poco, rare

hamburguesa.

helado, ice cream

helado de mantecado, custard ice cream

helado de nata, custard ice cream

helado de sobores variadas, mixed ice creams

helado quemado, bowl of ice cream topped with grilled sugar

helote, sweet corn-pudding ice cream

hervido, boiled, poached. This can also refer to a Venezuelan soup of
vegetables, spices and meat

hielo, ice

hielo, con, a drink "on the rocks"

hierba, herb

hierba buena, mint

hierba finas, chopped mixed herbs

hierba luisa, lemon-flavored herbal tea

higadillos, chicken livers

hígado, liver

hígado de ternera, calf's liver

hígado encebollado, liver and onions

higiditos, chicken livers

higo, fig. *Higos secos* are dried figs

higos a la Malagueña, figs, Málaga style.

hinojo, fennel

hojaldre, flaky or puff pastry

hojas de laurel, bay leaves

hojas de parra, vine leaves

hojiblanca, black olive

holandas, grape spirit

hongos, mushrooms

horchata, iced, creamy drink made with honey and almonds.
Sometimes made with tiny crushed artichokes known as tiger nuts.
In El Salvador, this is a rice-based sweet beverage (usually served in a
plastic bag). Watch out for the purity of the water. In Costa Rica, this is
a clear alcoholic beverage made from corn.
Be careful, this can be dangerous!

horchata de almendra, beverage made of ground almonds

hormiga culona, fried ants! Still found in Colombia

hormigas rojas, red ants (served live) with salt and lime.
Served in parts of Mexico *gracias, pero NO.*

hornazo, cake (served at Easter)/sausage-stuffed bread

horno, baked/oven

horno, al, baked/roasted

hortaliza, greens

hostería, informal restaurant, usually associated with an inn

huachinango, red snapper. *A la Veracruzana* (Veracruz style) with tomato
sauce, capers, green olives, onions and yellow peppers

huerta, with assorted vegetables

hueso, bone

hueso de santo, "bone of the saint":
candied egg yolk in an almond roll. It looks like a bone

huevas, fish roe/fish eggs

hielo.

hueso.

huevas prensadas, tuna roe/tuna eggs

huevo hilgado, garnish of shredded boiled eggs

huevos, eggs

huevos a la española, eggs stuffed with tomatoes
and served with a cheese sauce

huevos a la flamenca, eggs baked with tomatoes, vegetables and sausage

huevos al la madrileña, baked eggs with sausage and sliced tomato

huevos a la mexicana, scrambled eggs with onions and peppers

huevos al nido, rolls filled with tomato sauce and egg yolk and topped with
beaten egg whites, then baked

huevos al plato, fried eggs

huevos al salmorejo, baked eggs with asparagus, pork sausage and ham

huevos cocidos, hard-boiled eggs

huevos con tocino, eggs and bacon

huevos de mújol, Mediterranean caviar (grey-mullet roe)

huevos duros, hard-boiled eggs

huevos duros con mayonesa, hard-boiled eggs with mayonnaise

huevos escalfados, poached eggs

huevos estilo extremeña, vegetables with ham and eggs

huevos flamencos, see *huevos a la flamenca.* These "Gypsy eggs" are a
traditional dish from Seville and the ingredients vary greatly,
incorporating whatever is at hand

huevos fritos, fried eggs

huevos motuleños, *tortillas,* fried eggs, black beans, ham and tomato sauce.
A Mexican breakfast dish

huevos pasados por agua, soft-boiled eggs

huevos pericos, scrambled eggs

huevos poché, poached eggs

huevos por agua, soft-boiled eggs

huevos poché

huevos rancheros, fried eggs served with a hot tomato sauce; literally,
"ranchers' eggs," served to Mexican laborers in the morning. Today it is
served in the morning and as a snack at any time

huevos rellenos, deviled eggs

huevos revueltos, scrambled eggs

huit la coche, mushroom-like corn fungus

humita, In Chile, ground corn wrapped in a corn husk and boiled. Highly
seasoned. In Ecuador, this refers to a sweet-corn *tamale*

húngaros, spicy sausage found in Uruguay

infusiones, herbal teas

inglesa, a la, rare meat/served with boiled vegetables

intxaursalsa, A Basque walnut cream

IVA, (VAT) Value Added Tax. *IVA no incluido* means VAT not included

jabalí, boar

jaiba, Latin American crab

jalapeño, green, very hot pepper. Of the over 60 varieties of
chilies found in *Mexico*, this one is hot, but not murderously so

jalea, jelly

jamón, ham

jamón cocido, boiled ham

jamón de York, cooked ham on the bone

jamón en dulce, ham boiled and served cold

jamón gallego, smoked ham

jamón ibérico, cured ham

jamón serrano, thin slices of cured ham (like prosciutto)

japuta, pomfret (a deep-water fish). Means "son of a bitch"

jarabe, syrup of fresh fruit

jardinera, a la, served with vegetables

jarra, carafe/pitcher

jarrete, hock/shin bone

jengibre, ginger

jerez, sherry

jerez, al, braised in sherry

jerez almontillado, older *jerez fino*.
Aged at least eight years in wood
with a gold color and nutty flavor

jerez fino, pale dry sherry

jerez manzanilla, slightly sharper sherry than *jerez fino*

jerez oloroso, dark, full-bodied sherry.
Most are sweet. The best are dry

jerez palo cortado, a rare sherry, light and gold with a complex "character"

jerez seco, dry sherry

jeta, pig's cheek

jibia, cuttlefish

jícama, a root vegetable similar to a potato, usually eaten raw with sweet
tropical fruit found in Latin America

jitomate, tomato (in Latin America)

jobo, hogplum, a type of plum found in Puerto Rico. The fruit is oval, yellow
and a couple of inches long, and is usually used to make jelly

judías, dried beans

judías blancas, white beans

judías negras, black beans

judías rojas, red beans

judías verdes, green or string beans

judiones, broad beans

judiones de la granja, broad beans with sausage and pig's foot

jueye, land crab (in Puerto Rico)

jugo, juice/fruit juice/gravy

jugo de fruta, fruit juice

jugo de naranja, orange juice

jugo de pomelo, grapefruit juice

jugo de tomate, tomato juice

jugo, en su, in its own juice

juliana, with shredded vegetables

julivert, parsley

jurel, mackerel

kaki, persimmons

kirsch, cherry liqueur

kokotxas, Basque dish of tender glands near the throat of cod

kuchen, pie (a word used in parts of Latin America)

lacón, ham (boiled)/pork shoulder

lacón curado, salted pork

lamprea, lamprey (seafood)

lamprea de mer, eel

langosta, lobster

langosta a Arragón, lobster in a pepper sauce

langosta a la Catalana, lobster in a ham, mushroom and white sauce

langosta a la Costa Brava, lobster in tomato sauce

langosta a la vasca, lobster in a seafood sauce

langosta con pollo, lobster and chicken in a tomato stew

langostinos, shrimp/prawns

langostinos con clavo, shrimp in a clove-scented marinade

lapa, large roasted rodent! Found in Venezuela *NO, THANKS.*

lardo, lard

laurel, hojas de, bay leaves

lebrada de progonaos, rabbit stew in wine sauce

lebrato, rabbit

lechal/lechazo, milk-fed lamb

leche, milk

lechecillas de ternera, calf's sweetbreads

leche desnatada, skim milk

leche enter, whole milk

leche frita, creamy custard with a hard crust

leche manchada, milk with a dash of coffee

jugo de naranja y ron.

lamprea.

leche merengada/leche meringuada, cold milk with meringues (ice milk)

leche quemada, a Mexican dessert made of vanilla and sugar

lechón, pork

lechona, suckling pig in Latin America

lechón al horno, a Bolivian dish of roast pork with sweet potatoes

lechón asado/lechóna asada, roast suckling pig

lechosa, papaya

lechuga, lettuce

legumbres, vegetables

lengua, tongue

lengua de gato, "cat's tongue": thin, crisp cookies

lenguado, sole

lentejas, lentils

lentejas onubenses, lentils with spicy sausage and onions *lenguado.*

levadura, yeast/baking powder/any leavening agent

levadura quimica, baker's yeast

liadillos, stuffed meat/cabbage rolls

liba, sea bass

licor, liquor

licor de bellota, a liquor made from acorns

licor de petalos, rose-petal liquor

licuado, milk shake/fruit juices mixed with water

liebre, hare   *lima.*

lima, lime

limón, lemon

limonada, lemonade   *limón.*

lisa, grey mullet. In Venezuela, this can refer to tap beer

liscos, omelette with bacon

lista de platos, menu

lista de precios, list of prices

listo de vinos, wine list

liviano, light beverage

llagosta, lobster dish

llagosta a la catalona, crayfish with wine and chocolate

llamantol, lobster

The food on the western coast of South America has been heavily influenced by immigrants from the orient.

llapingacho, mashed potatoes with cheese (with a fried egg on top).
    A specialty in Ecuador

llauna, a la, baked

llegumet, beans, rice and potato dish

llenguado, sole

llet, milk

llimona, lemon

llobarro, bass

lluç, hake

lobarro, bass

locha, loach (carp)/cod

locrio de cerdo, pork and rice dish. A specialty in the Dominican Republic

locro, A Latin American corn and meat soup

lombarda, red cabbage

lomo, loin. *Lomito* is tenderloin

lomo a lo pobre, beef topped with two eggs, served with french fries. A Chilean dish

lomo bajo, sirloin

lomo curado, cured pork sausage

lomo de cerdo con leche, pork loin pot roast in milk

lomo embuchado, cured smoked pork loin

lomo montado, "mounted steak": tenderloin with two eggs on top and served with rice and fried bananas. A Bolivian specialty

lomo relleno, steak stuffed with spices and herbs (especially cilantro). A specialty in Panama

lomo saltado, stir-fried steak served with onions, rice, tomatoes and vegetables. A Peruvian specialty

lonch, lunch (you will sometimes see this on menus in Mexico)

lonchas de jamón, slices of cured ham

longaniza, long spicy sausage

lonja, thick slice of meat

lubina, sea bass

lubina albufera, sea bass with paprika sauce

lubina a la cantábrica, bass with white wine, lemon and garlic

lubina a la marinera, bass in a parsley sauce

lucia/lucio, pike

macarones/macarrones, macaroni

macarrones gratinados, macaroni and cheese

macedonia de frutas, fruit salad

machacón, boiled potato dish

machas, clams. A word used in Chile

macho, large green banana found in Latin America

madejas, lamb intestines

madrileña, a la, with tomatoes, sausage and paprika/with peppers

madrileño, with lemon and oil

maduro, ripe

magdalenas, spongecakes/muffins

machas.

magras con tomate, fried ham in a tomato sauce

magro, lean

magro con tomate, fried ham in tomato sauce

mahón, mild cheese

mahonesa, mayonesa, mayonnaise

maíz, corn

majarete, corn meal and custard dessert.
A specialty in the Dominican Republic

maiz.

maiz is arguably the most important food export of the western hemisphere.

málaga, sweet dessert wine

mallorquina, a la, highly
seasoned seafood

malta, malt beverage with barley,
sugar cane and hops (non-alcoholic).
Found in Puerto Rico. In Latin America, dark beer

malteada, milk shake

malvasia, sweet dessert wine

mamey, sweet red/orange tropical fruit
(mammee apple)

manchego, hard sheep's-milk cheese

mandarina, tangerine

mandioca, cassava, a starchy, boiled root served like mashed potatoes. Found
on menus in Paraguay

mango, mango. In southern Puerto Rico, the mangos have a flavor
similar to pineapples

maní (manises), peanut (peanuts)

manitas de cerdo, pig's feet

manitas de cordero, leg of lamb

manjar blanco, a soft toffee dessert found in Colombia and Peru

manojo, bunch/handful

manos de cerdo, pig's feet

manteca, butter in Argentina and Uruguay

mantecado, vanilla ice cream/small butter cake/creamy
cinnamon-flavored custard

mantega colorada, spicy pig's fat (usually spread on toast)

mantequilla, butter

manzana, apple

manzana en dulce, apple in honey

manzanas al horno, baked apples

manzanas asadas, baked apples

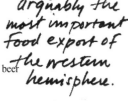

mantequilla

manzanilla, herbal tea (camomile tea)

manzanilla, pale dry sherry (slightly sharper than *jerez fino)*

manzanillas, green olives known as Seville olives

maracuya, passion fruit

margarina, margarine

margarita, tequila with lime juice

maria, whiting

mar i muntanya, a dish of shrimp and chicken

marinado, marinated

marinera, a la, This can mean many different
   things. Usually it means with tomatoes,
   herbs, onions and wine. Can also mean
   cooked with seafood in hot sauce

a la marinera means Sailor style.

mariscada, mixed shellfish/shellfish in a parsley, wine, olive oil
   and garlic sauce

mariscos, seafood. *Mariscos del día* means fresh seafood

marisquería, seafood restaurant that frequently has tanks of live seafood

mar i terra, chicken and seafood dish

marmitako, Basque tuna casserole

marquesa de chocolate, chocolate mousse

marquesita, chocolate confection

marrajo, shark

marrón, a large cup of strong coffee
   with a small amount of milk (in Venezuela)

marroncito, small cup of strong coffee
   with a small amount of milk (in Venezuela)

maruca, large cod

más, more

masa, pastry/dough/pasta. In Mexico, the corn dough used to make *tortillas*

matalahuga, matalahuva, anise

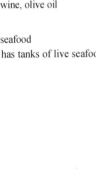

matambre, beef roll stuffed with vegetables

maté, caffeinated drink (found in Latin America)
   similar to tea and made from the leaves
   of a member of the holly family.

maté de coca, coca-leaf tea

mat mulo, very fresh

mavi, beer made from tree bark. Found in Puerto Rico

maté. is very bitter.

mayonesa, mayonnaise

mazamorra, thick meat and corn soup. A Colombian specialty

mazamorra morada, fruit pudding made from purple corn.
   A Peruvian specialty

mazapán, marzipan

mechada, although this can mean any number of things, it most often
   refers to a roast

medallones, medallions/small steaks/fish steaks

media/medio, half

media botella, half-bottle

media luna means half moon.

medialuna, breakfast croissant found in Argentina

mediana, a large bottle of beer

media noche, small, sweet bun glazed with egg/pork,
   ham and cheese sandwich found in Puerto Rico

mejillones, mussels

mejorana, marjoram

melaza, molasses

marjoram is closely related to oregano.

mel i mató, cream cheese with honey

melindres, marzipan biscuits

melocotón, peach

melón, melon

melón al calisay, melon with liquor poured on top

membrillo, quince

menestra, vegetable soup

menestra de Tudela, asparagus stew

menestra, as in minestrone.

menjar blanco, dessert with cream, lemon and ground almonds

menta, mint. *Menta poleo* is mint tea

menú, menu

menú de degustación, taster's menu

menú de la casa, often means fixed-price menu

menú del día, menu of the day

menú fijo, fixed-price menu

menú turístico, tourist menu (usually fixed price)

menudillos, chicken giblets

menudo, offal/tripe (the lining of an animal's stomach)

menudos gitanos, tripe with ham, garlic, saffron and cumin

merendero, an open-air snack bar

merengada, fruit juice, milk and sugar

merengues, meringues

Some people consider menudo to be a cure for hangovers.

merienda, snack. In Mexico, this is usually a late-evening snack

merlano, whiting (seafood)

merluza, cod or whiting

merluza a la castellana, cod with shrimp, clams, eggs and chili

merluza a la gallega, cod with potatoes and paprika

merluza a la koskera, a Basque dish of cod with clams

merluza a la madrileña, cod with ham and cheese, rolled in breadcrumbs
   and topped with tomato sauce

merluza a la vasca, cod in a white wine and parsley sauce

merluza en salsa verde, cod in a parsley sauce

mermelada, marmalade/jam

mero, grouper/perch/sea bass

mero a la levantina, grouper with
rosemary and lemon juice

mero.

mesa, table

mescal/mezcal, alcoholic beverage made from the agave (maguey) plant
(similar to tequila)

mesón, simple, local restaurant

mezclado, mixed

michelada, beer, ice and lime juice

michirones, beans stewed with chili peppers and sausage

miel, honey

mielga, a type of shark

miel y mató, honey over cream cheese

miera cielo, cod and red-pepper salad

migas, croûtons/sautéed breadcrumbs

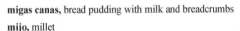

mielga.

migas canas, bread pudding with milk and breadcrumbs

mijo, millet

milanesa, breaded and fried veal cutlet

milanesa, a la, can mean either breaded and fried or served with cheese

milanesa de carne, sliced beef, breaded and then deep fried.
A specialty in Argentina

milanesa de pollo, slices of chicken, breaded and then deep fried.
A specialty in Argentina

milanesa res, breaded and fried steak

minuta, menu

minutas, honey-flavored drink made with crushed ice. Found in El Salvador

mistela, wine and grape juice

mixiotes, pieces of chicken served in a spicy sauce

mixto, mixed (can also mean a combination of meats)

mofongo, mashed and then roasted plantain with spices and *chicharrones.*
A specialty in the Dominican Republic and Puerto Rico

mogollas, wheat rolls with raisins

mojama, blue-fin tuna

mojara a la plancha, grilled ocean perch

mojarra, bream/fresh water fish/ bluegills

mojete, cod, peppers and onion salad/vegetable dip

mojo, a sauce with spicy peppers

mojo colorado, mixture of paprika, cumin and chili peppers

mojo isleño, Puerto Rican sauce of onions, olives, capers, tomatoes,
garlic and vinegar

muy sabroso!

mojojones, mussels

mole, thick, dark complex chili sauces invented in Mexico

mole poblano, chicken with sauce of chili pepper, chocolate and spices.

   Turkey is substituted for chicken in ***mole poblano de guajolote***

mole verde, green sauce with many ingredients including *tomatillos*

moll, red mullet

mollejas, sweetbreads. In Latin America, blood sausage

molusco, snail, mussel or clam (mollusk)

mondongo, seasoned tripe stew

mongetes/monjetes, dried white beans

montado, a type of canapé

montilia, a dry sherry

montilla, dessert wine

mora, blackberry

moraga de sardines, sardine casserole

morcilla, blood sausage/black pudding (made from blood, onions and rice)

morcilla de ternera, blood sausage made from calves' blood

morcilla dulce, sweet blood sausage. Popular in Uruguay

morcón, a spiced ham

morena, moray eel

moreno, almond meringue

morilla, morel mushroom

morena.

moro, "Moors." In Spanish-speaking countries, you'll find reference to ***moro*** or the Moors who dominated Spain for over 700 years. This term can

   mean many things, but frequently means a spicy sauce

moros y cristianos, black beans and white rice

morragote, grey mullet

morro, cheek

mortadela, salami

morteruelo, mixed-meat hash

moscatel, sweet dessert wine

mosh, oats with honey and cinnamon. A Guatemalan dish

mostachones, "S"-shaped biscuits

mostaza, mustard

mosto, grape juice

muchacho, beef loin roasted and served in a sauce. A specialty in Venezuela

mújol, grey mullet

musclos, chicken legs

muslo, drumstick of poultry

musola, a type of shark

muy hecho, meat well-done

muy seco, very dry

muslo.

muzzarella, mozzarella

nabo, turnip

nacatamales, *tortilla* filled with meat, corn and sauce and steamed in banana leaves or a corn husk. A Latin American dish

nachos, *tortilla* chips with *frijoles refritos,* grated cheese, *jalapeños, guacamole,* black olives and sour cream

ñame, yam in the Dominican Republic

naranja, orange.

Naranja agria (sour orange) is a common seasoning used in Mexico and Puerto Rico

naranjada, orangeade

naranjilla, citrus fruit juice (a cross between peach and orange)

nata, cream

nata batida, whipped cream

natillas, pudding/spiced custard

natural, raw or fresh

navajas, razor clams

navarra, a la, stuffed with ham

navidad, "Christmas": on a menu, this is a dish most likely served at Christmas

nécoras, spider crabs/sea crabs

nectarinas, nectarines

negrito, small cup of strong black coffee (in Venezuela)

nieves, sorbet (means "snow")

níscalo, wild mushroom

níspero, sapodilla (a rough-skinned, brown fruit from a tropical evergreen tree). Found in Puerto Rico

nixtamal, corn-meal dough

nopales, sliced and cooked cactus leaves

nopalito, cactus-leaf salad

ñoquis, the same as the Italian gnocchi (potato dumplings). Popular in Argentina

ñora, mild and sweet peppers

nueces, walnuts

nuez, nut

nuez moscada, nutmeg

oca, goose

ocopa, potatoes or eggs in a spicy sauce. A Peruvian specialty

oliaigua, water-based soup flavored with garlic, parsley and olive oil. A specialty in the Balearic Islands

olímpicos, club sandwiches found in Uruguay

olivas, olives

olla, stew. Named after the clay pot it's cooked in

olla de carne, Costa Rican beef stew, usually with plantains and yucca

olla de trigo, chickpea soup with sausage and bacon

olla gitana, thick vegetable stew

olla podrida (putrid pot), stew of meat, poultry, ham and vegetables

olleta, thick, chunky vegetable soup

oloroso, full-bodied sherry. Some are sweet. The best are dry

omelette, omelette

once, las, *Once* means eleven – *aguardiente* has eleven letters. So, when
   someone in Chile says that he is having his "*once*," it means that he is
   having a drink of *aguardiente*. *Once* also refers to snacks served in
   the late afternoon or early evening. Tea or coffee is served with cookies, toast, cheese or other small appetizers

oporto, port

orégano, oregano

oreja (de cerdo), pig's ear

orejones, dried apricots

ortellete, deep-fried pastry flavored with anise

ortiga, nettle

If you encounter the letter "O" on a menu it probably means "OR".

orujo, potent alcoholic beverage made from grapes

oscuro, dark (in color)

ostiones, small local oysters found in Puerto Rico and the Dominican
   Republic. In South America, this can refer to scallops

ostras, oysters

oveja, ewe

pa amb oli, bread with olive oil and often rubbed with garlic and tomato. A
   specialty in Mallorca. Specialties of Mallorca are found throughout
   South America

pa amb tomàquet, toast snack with tomato sauce, olive oil, ham and cheese

pabellón/pabellón criolla, shredded beef in a spicy tomato sauce with rice,
   plantains and beans. A specialty in Colombia and Venezuela

pacanas, pecans

pachamanca, stew of meat and vegetables cooked in clay pots. A specialty
   in Peru

pacharán, alcoholic beverage made from the blackthorn fruit (sloe)

pacumutu, In Latin America, beef on a skewer

pa d'ous, flan

paella, saffron-flavored rice with assorted seafood (or with meat). This Spanish
specialty is named after the *paellera*, the pan in which *paella* is made

paella a la catalana, *paella* with tomatoes, pork, sausage, squid, red peppers

paella a la marinera, *paella* with seafood

paella a la Valenciana, *paella* with fish and meat (usually assorted shellfish and chicken)

paella al estillo de Parellada/paella sin trabajo, *paella* without shells or bones

SIN Trabajo means without work

paella alicantina, *paella* with fish, onions, green peppers and tomatoes

paella castelana, *paella* with meat

paella huertana de Murcia, assorted-vegetable *paella*

paella marinera, *paella* with fish

paella negra, rice made black by cooking in squid ink

pagre, bream

paico, lemon- and anise-flavored *aguardiente*

paila, fried eggs with bread

pajaritos, small birds

pajuil, cashew

palacones de plátano, fried plantain

palaia petit, sole

paleta/paletillo, shoulder or breast

palitos, skewer

palmeras de hojaldre, puff-pastry dessert

palmitos, hearts of palm

palo cortado, sweet, rare sherry, light and golden with a complex "character"

paloma, pigeon

palometa, deep-water fish

palometa blanca, pompano

palometa negra, pomfret, a deep-water fish

palomitas, popcorn

palomitas means little doves.

palta, avocado

palta a la jardinera, avocado stuffed with vegetable salad

palta a rellena, avocado stuffed with chicken salad

pan, bread. ***Barra de pan*** is a loaf of bread

pana, liver

panaché de verduras, vegetable stew with mixed vegetables

pana de coco, coconut bread

pan a la Francesa, french toast

pan aléman, dark bread

panapen, breadfruit

pan blanco, white bread

panceta, bacon/pork belly

pancita, tripe } *you don't want to mix these two up!*
pancitos, rolls

pan con tomate, bread rubbed with tomato and sprinkled with olive oil

pan de agua, french bread

pan de azúcar, sugar dessert bread

pan de cebada, corn and barley bread

pan de coco, coconut bread

pan de centeno, rye bread

pan de higos, dried fig cake

pan de horno, baked bread

buena de pan.

pan de leche, a cream-topped muffin eaten at breakfast

pan de munición, chocolate-custard cake

pan de pernil, jellied ham

pan de pueblo, long bread loaf

pan dulce, sweet bread

panecicos, fried sweet puff-pastry dessert

panecillos, rolls/small loaves of bread

pan integral, whole-wheat bread

pan negro, dark bread

pan rallado, bread crumbs

panquemado, sugar-glazed bread

panqueques, pancakes

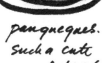
panqueques. Such a cute word, too!

panucho, deep fried *tortilla* filled with refried beans, meat, tomatoes, sour cream and onions

papa, potato

papas a la criolla, potatoes in a spicy sauce

papas a la huancaína, spicy potato dish with cheese and chili sauce. A specialty in Peru

papas arrugadas, spicy potato dish

papas bravas, potatoes in cayenne pepper

papas fritas, french fries/potato chips

papas rellenas, stuffed potatoes

papaya, papaya

papazul, *tortilla* filled with diced hard-boiled eggs and covered with a mild chili sauce popular on Mexico's Yucatán peninsula

parcha, passion fruit

pardet, grey mullet

pargo, sea bream/red snapper

parilla, a la, grilled

parilla criolla, marinated beef cooked on a grill

parillada, mixed charcoal grill of meats, including steak. In some Latin American countries, this often contains organ meats not often eaten in the United States and Canada. This can also refer to a selection of grilled fish

parillada mixta, mixed grill

parrochas, small sardines

pasa de corinto, currant

pasado, done, cooked

pasado bien, well-done

pasado poco, rare

pasas, dried fruit/raisins

parrochas.

pascua, "Easter": on a menu, this is a dish most likely served at Easter

pasta, pasta/soup noodles/can also mean pastry

pasta quebrada, a flaky pastry

pastel, pie/cake

pastel de choclo, a corn casserole filled with meats and vegetables. A specialty in Chile

pastel de higado, liver pâté

pastel de manzana, apple-mint crisp

pastel de pasas, raisin pudding

pastelería, pastry shop

pasteles, pastries

pastelillos, small tarts

pastelito, cookies/cupcakes

pastel murciano, veal pie

pastelón de vegetables, vegetable pastry

pastel vasco, filled sweet pastry

pastel.

pasticho, a dish which is very similar to lasagna. A specialty in Venezuela

pastilla, bar (as in candy bar) or small candy

pastor, al, usually means a pork-based dish

pata, foot

patacó, tuna casserole

patacones, In Ecuador, fried plantains with cheese. In Colombia, mashed potatoes and plantains

patacu, tuna casserole

patas de cordero, stewed leg of lamb

patatas, potatoes

patatas a la leonesa, potatoes with onions

patatas a la pescadora, potatoes with fish

patatas a la riojana, potato and sausage dish

patatas alli olli/patatas alioli, potatoes in garlic mayonnaise

We've never had tuna casserole anywhere but home, we're wondering if they put potato chips in theirs, too.

patatas bravas, spicy potatoes with paprika

patatas castellanas, potatoes and paprika

patatas fritas, french fries

patatas nuevas, new potatoes

patatas pobres, potatoes with garlic and parsley

patatas puré, mashed potatoes

patatas viudas, potatoes with fried onions

patatines, diced potatoes

patín, tomato-based sauce

patitos rellenos, stuffed duckling

pato, duck

pato a la naranja/pato a la servillana, duck à l'orange

pavías de pescado, fried fish sticks

pavipollo, large chicken

pavo, turkey

pavo relleno a la catalana, turkey with sausage, plum and pork stuffing

pavo trufado, turkey with truffle stuffing

pay, pie (you'll sometimes find this on menus in Mexico)

pazole, chicken or pork stew with chopped vegetables and herbs

pebre, oil and paprika sauce

pecho, breast/brisket

pecho de cerdo, pork belly

pecho de ternera, veal breast

pechuga, breast

pechuga de pollo, chicken breast

peix rei, whiting

peixina de pelegri, scallop

pellofa, Balearic Island drink of gin with ice, sugar and lemon

pelotas, meatballs

pepián, meat stew

pepinillo, pickle

pepino, cucumber

pepitas, sunflower seeds/pumpkin seeds

pepito, sautéed cutlet on a roll

pepitoria, stuffed with tomatoes, green peppers and onions/ fricassee.
This term has many meanings. For instance, *pepitoria de pollo*
is chicken with almonds

pequeño, small

pera, pear. *Peras al vino* are pears in a sweet wine sauce

perca, perch

percebes, shellfish/barnacle

perdices (perdíu), partridges (partridge)

perdices a la campesina, partridges with vegetables

perdices a la capellán, ham and pork sausage in a beef roll

perdices a la manchega, partridges cooked in red wine, peppers and herbs

perdices a la Torero, partridges with tomato, ham and anchovies

perdigones, partridges

perdiz, partridge

perejil, parsley

perifollo, chervil (an herb)

perilla, a type of bland cheese

pernil, ham/pork shoulder

perrito caliente, hot dog

perruñas/perruñillas, cinnamon cookies

pescadilla, whiting

pescadito, fried fish

pescado, fish

pescados y mariscos, fish and seafood

pestiños, sweet anise-flavored pastries

petit pois, peas (in some parts of Latin America)

peto, white-corn soup with milk. Found in Colombia

pez, fish

pez angel, angelfish shark

pez de San Pedro, John Dory fish (a firm-textured, white-fleshed fish with a mild, sweet flavor and low fat content)

pez espada, swordfish

pez limón, amberjack

pez martillo, hammerhead shark

pez plata, argentine (a fish similar to salmon)

píbil, dark sauce

picada, thick sauce of garlic, almonds, pine nuts, parsley and saffron

picadilla, creamy almond dressing

picadillo, ground meat/marinated pork and potatoes. In Latin America, this refers to snacks. In Mexico, this is a spicy seasoned ground-meat dish (served as either a main course or as a filling)

picado, ground up

picante, spicy/hot

picante de pollo, fried chicken served with fried potatoes and rice. Very spicy! *Picantes* can also refer to chicken or shrimp served in a spicy red sauce

picarones/picarrones, deep-fried sweet-potato batter served with syrup. A dish found in Peru

picata, pounded ingredients used to thicken sauces (see *picada*)

picatostes, fried, sugared and buttered toast

pichón, pigeon

pichón con pasas y piñones, pigeon with raisins and pine nuts

pichoncillo, young pigeon, squab

pichuncho, *pisco* and vermouth

pico de gallo, tomato, onion, cilantro and scallion relish (*salsa*)

picoso, hot, spicy

pie (pies), foot (feet)

pierna, leg (of beef)

pijama, caramel custard with ice cream topped with whipped cream

pijotas, baby cod

pijotas, small whiting

pil-pil, al, prepared with oil and garlic

pil-pilando, any dish served sizzling hot

piloncillo, raw sugar

pilongas, dried chestnuts

pilotas, meatballs

pimentón, paprika/cayenne pepper

pimienta de cayena, cayenne pepper

pimienta inglesa/pimienta jamaica, allspice

pimienta/pimienta negra, black pepper

pimiento, bell pepper

pimiento morrón, sweet red bell pepper

pimiento.

pimienton, paprika

pimientos de padrón, fried baby green peppers

pimientos de piquillo rellenos, fried red peppers, stuffed (often with cod)

pimientos fritos, deep-fried green peppers

pimientos rellenos, stuffed peppers

piña

pimientos rojos asados, roasted red-pepper salad

pimientos verde, green peppers

piña, pineapple

piña colada, rum mixed with pineapple juice and cream of coconut

pinchitos, snacks, appetizers/kebabs

pincho moruno, meat kebab. *Pincho de lomito* is tenderloin shish kebab

pinchos, snacks served on a toothpick/a dish similar to shish kebab, almost always served with meat. This is a specialty in Honduras. This is also the Basque word for *tapas*

pinocillo, alcoholic beverage made from toasted seeds

piñon, pine nut

piñonata, pine-nut cake

pinonos, a mixture of ground beef and plantains dipped in batter then fried

pintada, guinea hen

pintarroja, small shark

piparrada, a Basque word for dishes containing tomatoes and green peppers

piparrada vasca, tomato and pepper stew with ham

pipas, seeds

piperita, peppermint

pipián, hot chili sauce. In the Dominican Republic, this is a stew containing the intestine of a goat

pipirrana, salad of hard-boiled eggs, tomatoes, peppers, onions, tuna, ham, olive oil and garlic

pique a lo macho, chopped beef served with onions and vegetables.

piquete, meat, vegetables and potatoes in a hot-pepper sauce.

piragua, "snow cone" of ice topped with guava or tamarind syrup. A Puerto Rican dessert

piriñaca, chopped vegetable salad which often contains tuna

pisco, colorless and potent alcoholic beverage made from corn or grapes (often mixed with orange juice), found in Latin America. In Ecuador, it is similar to white rum. *Piscola* is *pisco* and coca-cola

pisco sour, lemon juice, sugar and *pisco* shaken together over ice and topped with beaten egg whites. A specialty in Ecuador

piso, fried vegetables

pistachio, pistachio nut

pistiñes, sweet anise-flavored fritters

pisto, mixed vegetable, tomato and zucchini salad

pisto manchego, ratatouille/zucchini, tomato and onion stew

pixin, monkfish

plancha (a la plancha)/planchada, grilled

generally, anything "a la plancha" is grilled.

plátanos, plantains. This vegetable looks like a banana, but it is picked when green. Unlike a banana, it's never eaten raw

plátanos flameados, plantains flambéed

plátanos fritos, fried plantains

plátanos horneados, baked plantains

platija, flounder

plato, dish/plate

plato combinado, combination plate

plato de hoy/plato del día, plate of the day

plato montañero, a Colombian dish with ground beef, sausage, salt pork, beans, rice, avocado and fried egg. This dish is also called *bandeja paisa*

plato típico, any dish which is "typical" to the region or country.

In Nicaragua, a large and inexpensive meal containing any of the
following: beans, rice, meat, fried bananas, *tortillas*, cheese and a salad

platos combinados, combination plates

plegonero, cod/whiting

poblano, green pepper. Not as hot as a *jalapeño*

pochas, beans

pochas a la riojana, black beans in a tomato sauce with sausage and meat

pocillo, strong black coffee served after dinner in Puerto Rico

poco hecho, rare

poco cocido, rare

poco pasado, rare

poleo, mint

poleomenta, mint tea

pollito, young chicken

pollo, chicken

pollo a la chilindrón, sautéed chicken with tomatoes, peppers and olives

pollo a la mexicana, Mexican-style chicken cooked with onions, green chili
peppers and tomatoes, usually served with rice and beans

pollo al canario, lemon and chicken. A popular dish in the Canary Islands

pollo al chilindrón, cooked chicken with onions, tomatoes and peppers

pollo asado, roast chicken

pollastre amb gambes, chicken in brandy sauce with shrimp *borracho means drunk.*

pollo borracho, fried chicken in a tequila-based sauce

pollo campurriano, rice with bacon, chicken, shallots and peppers

pollo en arroz, chicken and rice

pollo en cacerola, chicken casserole

pollo en chanfaina, chicken cooked with onions, tomatoes and peppers

pollo en pepitoria, chicken in a wine, garlic and saffron sauce

pollo pibil, chicken simmered in spices. In Mexico, marinated chicken
grilled in banana leaves

pollo reina clamart, roasted chicken with vegetables

pollo villeroy, breaded and fried chicken breast in a white sauce

polvorones, hazelnut and/or almond cookies

pomelo, grapefruit

ponche, punch (usually with brandy)

ponche crema, Venezuelan eggnog

pop, octopus

porc, pork

porcíon, small helping/portion

por favor, please

porotos, kidney beans

pop.

porra antequerana, *gazpacho* with ham or tomatoes

porrón, a glass from which you pour wine into your mouth from a distance of at least a foot

porrosaldo/porrusaldo, Basque potato and leek (and usually cod) soup

por unidad, per item

postre de músic, raisin, nut and wine dessert

postres, desserts

potaje, vegetable soup/thick soup (like chowder)

pote asturiana, bean and sausage soup

pote con coles, thick cabbage soup

poti poti, salt-cod salad with peppers and potatoes

pozole, corn and meat stew with hominy

preserva, preserve

primer plato, starter/first course

pringadas, fried bread with garlic. After the bread is fried in olive oil and garlic, sausage and ham are served on top. Fattening and delicious!

propina, tip. *No incluyen* (or ***incluido***) *propina* means tip not included

provoleta, provolone cheese

pucherete al estilo montañes, spicy blood-sausage stew

puchero, stew. In Uruguay, beef with beans, vegetables, sausage and bacon

puchero bogotana, boiled vegetables, meat and potatoes. A Colombian dish

puchero canario, meat and chickpea casserole. A Canary Islands specialty

pudín, pudding. ***Pudín de arroz,*** rice pudding

puerco, pork

puerco chuk, pork stew

puerro, leek

pulga, filled roll

pulpeta, slice of meat

pulpito, baby octopus

pulpo, octopus

pulpo a fiera a la gallega/pulpo de fiera, octopus with paprika and olive oil

pulque, alcoholic beverage distilled from the pulp of the agave (maguey) plant. It is much thicker than tequila, which is also from the agave plant

punta de diamante, diamond-shaped meringue cake

punta de espárrago, asparagus tip

puntas de filete de res, beef steak (usually sirloin tips) with guacamole and beans. A Mexican dish

puntillitas, small squid

punto, a, medium-done

punto, en su, medium-done

punto de nieve, whipped cream with beaten egg whites

(handwritten note: We don't know how poti poti tastes but we like the name.)

(handwritten note: puerro.)

pupusa, fried *tortillas* filled with cheese, beans and/or meat. You will find
   pupusas and *pupuserías* (snack stands selling *pupusas*) everywhere in
   El Salvador. In Honduras, *pupusas* are almost always filled with pork

puré de patatas/puré de papas, mashed potatoes

purée de apio, celery root which is boiled, puréed and served with salt and
   butter. Some think it tastes like chestnuts

puro de caña, alcoholic beverage made from sugar cane

purrusalda, Basque potato and leek (and usually cod) soup

queimada, apple, brandy, sugar and lemon drink

quemada, topped with caramelized cream

queque, cake

quesada, cheesecake (a dessert made with cheese, honey and butter)

quesadilla, cheescake. In Mexico, grilled or fried *tortilla* filled with meat,
   cheese, potatoes and/or chilies

quesillo, steamed *flan*. This can also refer to cheese

quesillo de leche y piña, milk and pineapple flan found in the Dominican
   Republic

queso, cheese

queso blanco, white cheese

queso de burgos, soft, white, creamy cheese

queso de cabrales, blue cheese (not as strong as Roquefort)

queso de camerano, goat's-milk cheese

queso de Cantabria, mild cheese made from cow's cream

queso de cervera, soft sheep's-milk cheese

queso de hoja, mild soft cheese from Puerto Rico

queso de Idiazábal, strong, creamy, smoky cheese

queso de mahón, semi-hard, tangy cheese

queso de mató, goat's-milk cheese

queso de oveja, mild sheep's-milk cheese

queso de pasiego, fresh soft cheese

queso de pichón, creamy blue cheese

queso de puzol, fresh cow's-milk cheese

queso de Roncal, strong, creamy sheep's-milk cheese (low-fat)

queso de San Simón, strong, smoky cheese

queso de tetilla, pungent, creamy white cheese made from cow's milk

queso de Tresviso-Pícon, a blue cheese

queso de villalón, soft cheese made from sheep's milk

queso del país, local cheese

queso fresco, white cheese (similar to feta cheese)

queso fundido, baked cheese dip

queso gallego, a creamy cheese

queso Ibores, goat's-milk cheese with a paprika-coated rind

queso majorero, goat cheese from the Canary Islands

queso manchego, hard, salty, rich and nutty cheese

queso zamorano, sheep's-milk cheese similar to *queso manchego*

quilet, bream

quinto, a small bottle of beer

quisquilla, shrimp

raba, breaded, fried squid

rábano, radish. *Rabanitos* are small radishes found in Latin America

rábano picante, horseradish

rabo, tail

rabo de buey/rabo de toro, oxtail

racimo, bunch (as in a bunch of grapes)

raciónes, large portion (usually of snacks)

ración piqueña on a menu means small portion.

raf, a type of tomato

ragout, ragoût

raíz, root

rajas, slices. In some parts of Latin America, grilled green peppers

rallado, grated

rama, dried hot chili peppers

ramillo, spicy

rana, ancas de, frog legs

rancho canario, stew of sausage, bacon,
      beans, potatoes and pasta. A specialty in the Canary Islands

rap/rape, monkfish/angler fish

raspas de anchoas, deep-fried backbones of anchovies

ravioles, ravioli

raya, ray, skate (seafood)

rebanada, slice

I'll pass.

rebozado, coated with breadcrumbs and fried

recargo, extra charge

redondo, filet of beef

refrescos, soft drink/cool drink. In Costa Rica, fruit shakes. In Puerto Rico,
      you will find *refrescos del país* signs everywhere, often automobile trunks
filled with fruit juices, especially *cocos fríos* (cold drinking coconuts)

refrito, refried

refritos, refried beans

regular, meat done medium

rehogado, sautéed

rellenas/os, stuffed/filled

rellenos de papa, meat-stuffed potatoes fried in batter

remanat d'ous, scrambled eggs

rémol, brill/flounder

remolachas, beets

reo, sea trout

repollo, cabbage

remolachas.

repostería de la casa, house-specialty desserts

requemado, cold rice pudding with sugar topping

requesón, cottage cheese

res, beef

reserva, mature wine (of older vintage)

reserva especial, wine of an exceptional vintage. A step above *gran reserva*

revoltillo, scrambled eggs

revueltos, scrambled eggs

revuelto mixto, scrambled eggs with vegetables

riñón, kidney

riñonada, roasted kidneys

riñones al jerez, kidneys cooked in sherry

rioja, a red wine similar to Bordeaux. Rioja is a wine-growing region of
   Spain

rioja, a la (a la riojana), served with red peppers

róbalo, haddock/snook

robioles, custard-filled pastry

rocoto, a hot red pepper

rodaballo, turbot/flounder

rollitos, small filled rolls

rollo de carne, meat loaf

rollo de merluza, cod roll in a parsley sauce

romana, a la, dipped in batter and then fried

romero, rosemary

romesco/romescu, mild, sweet chili pepper. This can also refer to a sauce of
   peppers, tomatoes, ground almonds and hazelnuts

romesco de pescado, mixed fish. *Romesco de peix* is a fish stew

ron, rum

ronyon, kidney

ropa vieja, left-over meat and vegetables cooked
   with tomatoes and green peppers. In Panama, rice
   covered with spicy shredded beef and green peppers

ropa vieja means old clothes.

rosada, shark

rosado, rosé wine

rosbif, roast beef

rosca/rosco, doughnut

roscon, roll filled with guava jelly and coated with sugar

roscon de reyes, sweetened bread, coated with sugar and candied fruits. A holiday bread with a "charm" hidden inside

rosé, rosé wine

rosquilla, doughnut (usually glazed)

rossejat, cooked rice dish

rostit, roasted

rovellon, wild mushroom

rubio, red mullet

ruibarbo, rhubarb

ruso, cake with custard filling

sábalo, shad (seafood)

sacarina, saccharin

sacromonte, omelette made of eggs, vegetables, brains and bull's testicles. A specialty of Granada

saice, a spicy meat broth

sajta, chicken served in *aji* (hot pepper) sauce. A Bolivian specialty

sal, salt

saladitos, appetizers

salado, salted

salazón, cured (salted fish or meat)

salchicha, pork sausage

Sabores or Sabroso means Savory or tasty.

salchichas blancas, pork sausage with fried onions

salchichas de Frankfurt, hot dogs, frankfurters

salchichón, salami (cured sausage)

salema, bream

salmó, salmon

salmón, salmon

salmón ahumado, smoked salmon

salmón a la ribereña, fried salmon steaks

salmonete, red mullet

Salmón

salmonete en papillote, red mullet cooked in foil

salmorejo, thick sauce of bread, tomatoes, vinegar, green peppers, olive oil and garlic. A variation of *gazpacho*

salmorejo cordobes, chilled *gazpacho*

salmorreta, a smoky tomato sauce

salmuera, in brine

salon de té, tea room

salones, cured lamb or beef

salpicón de mariscos, mixed shellfish salad

salsa, sauce. In Mexico, relish of chopped tomatoes, onions, cilantro and scallions; also called *pico de gallo*, **salsa crud**, or **salsa fresca**

salsa bechamel, white sauce/béchamel sauce

salsa criolla, spicy sauce used on steaks in Uruguay

salsa de tomate, ketchup/tomato sauce

salsa española, sauce with wine, spices and herbs

salsa hollandaise, hollandaise sauce

salsa ingles, Worcestershire sauce

salsa mayordoma, butter and parsley sauce

salsa picante, hot-pepper sauce

salsa ranchero, red chili sauce with a tomato base

salsa romesco, sauce with tomatoes and garlic or ground nuts and
sweet peppers

salsa tártara, tartar sauce

salsa verde, parsley sauce. In Mexico, chilies, cilantro, garlic and green
tomato sauce. In Latin America, hot sauce with tomatoes and peppers

salsifí, salsify

salteado/a, sautéed

salteño, turnover filled with meat and sauce

salvado, bran

salvia, sage

sama de pluma, bream

samfaina, sauce of eggplant, zucchini, peppers, onions and tomatoes

sancochado, meat and vegetable stew with spices

sancocho, vegetable soup with meat or fish. In the Canary Islands this is
white fish and boiled potatoes

sancocho canario, fish stew with potatoes in a red-pepper sauce

sandía, watermelon

sandwich, sandwich

sandwich caliente, hot sandwich.
In Uruguay, a grilled ham and cheese sandwich

sandwich mixto, often refers to a ham and cheese sandwich

sangre, blood

sangría, chilled red wine, fruit juice, brandy and soda. There are many vari-
ations. For example, in Ecuador, red wine, sugar, fruit and lemon juice

sangrita, tequila with lime, orange and tomato juice

santiaguiño, (clawless) lobster

sard, bream

sardinas, sardines

sargo, bream

sarsuela, fish stew (see also *zarzuela*)

sarten, en, from the frying pan

schop, In Chile, beer (usually draft beer)

sebo, fat

seco, dry. Can also refer to dry wine

seco de, stew

seco de cordero, lamb stew

seco de gallina, chicken stew

segundo plato, second course

semi-dulce, semi-sweet

semifríos, molded frozen dessert

semillas, seeds

sémola/semolina, ground duram wheat

sencillo, plain

sepia, cuttlefish

sequillos, hazelnut meringues

serenata, fish in vinaigrette with onions, avocados and vegetables.
A specialty in Puerto Rico

serrano, thin slices of cured ham (like prosciutto). This also refers to a
small green chili pepper that is hotter than a *jalapeño*

servicio, service

servicio incluido, service included (tip included)

servicio no incluido, service not included (tip not included)

servilleta, napkin

sesamo, sesami. Can also refer to perch

sesos, brains   *No me gusta!*

seta, mushroom.
This can also refer to a mushroom or oyster grilled with garlic

setas a la bordalesa, mushrooms cooked in red wine and onions

setas salteadas, mushrooms with sausage and garlic

seviche, cold whitefish salad popular in Acapulco, Mexico. *See* **ceviche**

sevillana, a la, cooked in wine with olives

shangurro, stuffed crab

sidra, alcoholic cider

sifón, soda water

silpancho, beef (thinly sliced, breaded and fried) served with an egg on top

sin, without

sincronizadas, flour tortilla (folded and browned) with ham and cheese

singani, Bolivian alcoholic beverage made from grapes

sin gas, without carbonation

sin trabajo, seafood served with the shells removed (means "no work")

sobrasada, soft *chorizo* (sausage) often used as a spread

sobrebarriga, breaded and stuffed steak

soda blanca, soda water

sofregit, sauteed onions and tomatoes

sofreído, sauteed

sofrito, onions fried with garlic/sautéed. In Puerto Rico, sauté of tomatoes, onions, red and green peppers, spices, garlic and cilantro. Commonly found in stews and bean dishes

soja, soy

soldaditos, fried fish sticks

soldaditos de pavia, fried strips of salt cod

soldat, sole

solla, plaice

solo, neat (straight-up) alcoholic beverage

solomillo, fillet steak/tenderloin/sirloin

solomillo andaluz, pork tenderloin

sol y sombra, brandy and anise-flavored liquor (means "sun and shade")

sooyosopy, Paraguayan soup of cornmeal and ground meat, usually served with rice

sopa, soup

SooyoSopy is a Guaraní word. Guaraní is the other official language of Paraguay.

sopa a la criolla, spicy noodle and beef soup. A Peruvian specialty

sopa al cuarto de hora, clam, ham, shrimp and rice soup. The ingredients vary greatly as it is a soup you can make with whatever you have on hand "in a quarter of an hour"

sopa al estilo Mallorca, cabbage soup

sopa alpurrañas, egg and ham soup

sopa cachorreñas, fish soup with orange zest, vinegar and oil

sopa castellana, vegetable soup/garlic soup with cumin.

sopa clara, consommé

sopa criolla dominicana, a soup of stewed meat, greens, onions, spices and pasta. A specialty in the Dominican Republic

sopa de ajo, garlic soup

sopa de ajo blanco, cold soup of garlic, grapes and ground almonds *ajo .*

sopa de alubrias negras, thick black-bean soup

sopa de albóndigas, chicken broth with meatballs

sopa de almendras, almond pudding

sopa de aragonesa, soup of calf's liver and cheese, topped with bread or cheese crust

sopa de calabaza, squash soup

sopa de calducho, clear soup

sopa de cangrejos, crab bisque

sopa de cebolla, onion soup

calabaza

sopa de cocido, meat soup

sopa de cola de buey, oxtail soup

sopa de dátiles, brown-mussel soup

sopa de fideos, noodle soup

sopa de frutas de mar, shellfish soup

sopa de galets, pasta and meatball soup

sopa de gallina, chicken soup

sopa de gato, garlic soup with grated cheese

sopa de guisantes, pea soup

sopa de habichuelas negras, black-bean soup

sopa de la cena, pork-sparerib soup

sopa de lentejas, lentil soup   *lima.*

sopa de lima, chicken and lime soup

sopa de maní, roasted-peanut soup

sopa de mariscos, shellfish soup. In Mexico, tomato and seafood chowder

sopa de mejillones, mussel soup

sopa de mondongo, tripe stew or soup

sopa de pasta, noodle/pasta soup

sopa de pescado, fish soup

sopa de picadillo, egg and ham soup

sopa de servillana, spicy fish soup flavored with mayonnaise   *tomat*

sopa de tomate, tomato soup

sopa de tortilla, Mexican soup of fried *tortilla* strips, chicken and chilies

sopa de tortuga, turtle soup   *verduras.*

sopa de verduras, vegetable soup

sopa de vino, soup containing sherry

sopa del quarto de hora, soup with a base of fried onions and rice

sopa espesa, thick soup

sopa liquida, "wet soup" or what we think of as soup. See **sopa seca**

sopa mahimones, soup with olive oil, bread and garlic base

sopa maimones, soup with olive oil, bread and garlic base

sopa mallorquina, thick soup of tomatoes, meat, eggs, onions and peppers

sopa mondongo, tripe stew   *No THANKS.*

sopa paraguaya, "Paraguayan soup" of mashed corn bread, cheese, onion,
   milk and eggs

sopa seca, rice or pasta covered with a sauce and served after soup in
   Mexico (means "dry soup"). The second course of a full meal

sopa servillana, spicy fish and mayonnaise soup

sopaipillas, fried pumpkin

sopapilla, deep-fried pastry   *— yes please.*

sope, Mexican dish of *tortillas* sealed together and filled with meat or cheese
   and fried

112

sorbete, sorbet/cold fruit drink. In Central America, this can refer to ice cream

sospiros de Moros, dry meringues

suave, soft

sucre, sugar

suero, whey

suflé, soufflé

Sospiro means Sigh - Sospiros de Moros means Moor's Sighs -

sugerencias del chef, chef's recommendations

suizos, breakfast rolls baked with sugar

supremas de rodaballo, thin slices of fish

suquet, fish stew

surrullitos, deep-fried corn sticks stuffed with cheese

surtido, assorted

surubí, a fresh-water fish similar to catfish found in Paraguay

suspiros, dry meringues. In Peru, sweet meringue dessert filled with cream and often with fudge

suspiros de monja, soft meringue with custard

susquet, assorted fish and shellfish stew

susquillo de pescador, assorted fish and shellfish stew

taberna, tavern

table, a platter of cheese or meat

taco, meat-filled *tortilla* with tomatoes, onions, and other ingredients.
  Dorado means a fried ("U"-shaped, crisp) *taco,*
  and *suave* means plain (not fried)

un taco.

tajada, slice. In Latin America, fried banana slices

tajaditas, fried banana chips

tallarines, noodles

tallarines a la italiana, tagliatelle

tamale, corn-meal dough filled with meat and sauce and steamed while wrapped in banana leaves or a corn husk. In Costa Rica, olives, rice and raisins are often included

tamarindo, tamarind

tapa, snack/appetizer.
  Tapa is the Spanish word for lid or cover.
  The bartender will place an appetizer on
  top of your glass of wine or beer

Tapas are frequently nuts, olives or meatballs.

tapado, stew

taronja, orange

tarragón, tarragon

tarrina, en, served in an earthenware pot

tarta, tart

tarta alaska, baked Alaska

tarta al whisky, whisky and ice-cream cake

tarta de almendra, almond cake

tarta de arroz, cake containing rice

tarta de manzana, apple tart

tarta de naranja, orange-almond cake

tarta de piñones, pine-nut cake

tarta de Santiago, almond cake

tarta helada, layered ice-cream cake

tartaletas, tartlets

tarta moca, mocha cake

tarta Pasiega, anise-flavored cheesecake

tartar crudo, steak tartare

tasca, a bar serving *tapas*

taza, cup

té, tea

una taza de té.

tecla de yema, candied egg-yolk pastries

té con leche, tea with milk

té con limón, tea with lemon

té helado, iced tea

tejas, egg-white, almond and sugar biscuits

tejos de queso, cheese pastries

tembleque, coconut pudding

tenca, tench (a Eurasian fish)

tenedor, fork

tepezcuintle, a Mayan specialty, the largest member of the rodent family

tepín, small, very hot chili pepper

tequeños, fried appetizer of dough
    wrapped around white cheese

tequila, ever had a *tequila* hangover? An alcoholic beverage distilled from
    the pulp of the agave (maguey) plant. Mexican *tequila* is often higher
    proof than *tequila* sold in the United States and Canada.

Four types are: **anejo** (aged in oak barrels for at least
    one year), **gold** or **joven abocado** (unaged
    with color and flavor added), **plata** or **blanco**
    (unaged and sold within two months of distilling)
    and **reposado** (aged from two months to
    one year, means "rested")

tercio, large bottle of beer

tereré, *maté* made with cold water

término medio, medium

ternasco, baby lamb

Tequila.

ternasco asado, lamb roasted in wine and lemons

ternera, veal

ternera a la estremeña, veal cooked in a sauce of onions, *chorizo* and sweet peppers

ternera a la sevillana, sautéed veal with sherry and green olives

terrina, pâté

tetería, tea shop

tetilla, a mild, creamy cheese

tiempo, al, at room temperature (*del tiempo* means "of the season")

tigres, mussels in cayenne-pepper sauce

tila, lime-flavored tea

tinto, black coffee in Colombia

tinto de verano, "summer red," red wine with lemon-lime soda water

tinto, vino, red wine

tío pepe, a type of sherry

tioro, Basque fish soup

típico de la región, regional specialty

tiradito, fish, lime juice and oil served with pepper sauce.

VINO TiNTo!

tisanas, herbal teas

tocinillo de cielo/tocino de cielo, very rich crème caramel

tocino, bacon

tocino de cielo, lemon-or cinnamon-flavored baked custard

todo incluido, all inclusive (price and service)

tojunto, rabbit, meat and vegetable stew

tomaquets, tomatoes

tomate, tomato

tomates rellenos, stuffed tomatoes

tomatillo, mild green fruit (similar to a green tomato)

tombet, vegetable stew

tomillo, thyme

tónic/tónica, tonic

tonyina, tuna

tordo, thrush

toro, bull

toronja, grapefruit

torrada, toast

torrados, toasted chickpeas

toro!

torreja/torrija, French toast/bread dipped in milk, fried and sugar coated

torta, cake/breakfast roll topped with sugar. In Costa Rica, meat and/or cheese sandwich. In Mexico, a sandwich

torta de aceite, plain, bland biscuit

torta de cielo, almond spongecake ("cake of heaven")

torta de hojaldre, puff pastry with jam

torta del casar, soft and creamy sheep's-milk cheese

torta de plátano, plantain and cheese cake

torta de Santiago, almond cake

torta milanesa, deep-fried meat sandwich

torta real, "royal cake" with eggs, almonds and cinnamon

tortell, breakfast roll with crushed almonds and lemon filling

tortilla, in Mexico, a flat, round, cooked unleavened bread. Corn *tortillas* are the daily starch of Mexico, made of *masa* (corn flour). In Northern Mexico, *tortillas* are often made with flour. In Spain, an egg omelette

tortilla a la catalana, omelette with sausage and beans

tortilla a la flamenca, Spanish omelette (see *huevos a la flamenca*)

tortilla a la jardinera, omelette with mixed vegetables

tortilla a la paisana, omelette with mixed vegetables

tortilla aliada, omelette with mixed vegetables

tortilla asturiana, tuna, onion and tomato omelette

tortilla a su gusto, omelette made with whatever ingredients you want

tortilla con quesillo, fried corn *tortilla* with melted cheese

tortilla de escabeche, omelette containing fish

tortilla de harina, flour *tortilla*

tortilla de huevos, omelette

tortilla de jámon, an omelette with ham

tortilla de patatas, potato omelette

tortilla española, omelette with potato and onion filling

tortilla francesa, plain omelette

tortilla gallega, omelette with sausage and peppers

tortilla granadina, omelette with brains, asparagus, peppers and artichokes

tortilla guisada, omelette with tomato sauce

tortilla hormigos, omelette with fried bread crumbs

tortilla murciana, omelette with tomato and red peppers

tortilla paisana, omelette with sausage, potatoes, peppers and tomatoes

tortilla piperrada, red pepper, onion and tomato omelette

tortilla sacromonte, omelette made of eggs, vegetables, brains and bull's testicles. A specialty of Granada *gross.*

tortillitas, pancakes

tortita, waffle

tortuga, turtle

tosta, toast with topping

tostada, toast. In Mexico, a fried *tortilla* topped with ingredients such as chicken, beans and/or cheese. In Venezuela, a sandwich with crisp bread, meat, cheese or chicken

tostadas de maíz, corn pancakes

tostaditas, Mexican *tortilla* chips. They can also refer to small *tostadas*

tostado, toasted. *Pan tostado* is toast

tostón, suckling pig

tostones, fried plantains

totopos, Mexican *tortilla* chips

tournedó, filet steak

toyina, salted tuna

trasero, rump

trigo, wheat

triguillo, turnip soup

tripas, tripe

trozo, rack (as in rack of lamb)

trucha, trout

trucha a la montañesa, trout cooked with white wine and bay leaves

trucha a la Navarra, trout baked with red wine and herbs and often wrapped in bacon

trucha frita a la asturiana, trout floured and fried in butter

trucha molinera, trout floured and fried with butter and lemon

trufa, truffle. *Trufado* means with truffles

truita, omelette. Can also mean trout

trumfes, potatoes

ttoro, Basque fish soup

tubo, a large glass of beer

tuétano, bone marrow

tumbet, vegetable casserole featuring eggplant

tuna, prickly pear

tuntas, freeze-dried potatoes

turrón, nougat. *Turrón de guirlache* is almond brittle

txacoli/txakoli, Basque white wine

txangurro, Basque dish of seasoned crabmeat

ulloa, a soft cheese similar to camembert

unidad, por, per item

urta, sea bream

urta a la roteña, baked bream in an onion, tomato and brandy sauce

utensilio, utensil

uvas, grapes

uvas pasas, raisins

vaca (carne de), beef

vaca salada, corned beef

vaina, a sweet sherry-based drink found in Chile

trucha.

uvas.

vainilla, vanilla

vainitas, Latin American word for green beans

valenciana, a la, usually means with tomatoes, rice and garlic

vapor, steamed

variada, bream

variado, assorted

vasca, a la, usually means in a garlic, parsley and white-wine sauce

vaso, glass/tumbler

vedella, veal

vegetales, vegetables

vegeteriano, vegetarian. In some parts of Latin America, *"no tiene carne"*
(literally "does not contain meat") means does not have beef, but may
contain other meat

venado, venison

veneras, scallops

venta, country inn serving food

veracruzana, a la, (Veracruz, Mexico style) with tomato sauce, capers,
green olives, onions and yellow peppers

verat, mackerel

verde, green/a common, green, medium-hot pepper

verduras, green vegetables

vermut (vermú), vermouth

vi, the Catalan word for wine

vi blanc, the Catalan word for white wine

vi negre, the Catalan word for red wine

vi novell, new wine, similar to Beaujolais Nouveau

vi rosat, the Catalan word for rosé wine

vieira, scallop

villeroy, chicken breasts or prawns coated in béchamel

vinagre, vinegar

vinagreta, vinaigrette

vino, wine

vino añejo, mature wine

vino blanco, white wine

vino clarete, rosé wine

vino común, table wine

vino de aguja, slightly sparkling white or rosé wine

vino de jerez, sherry

vino de la casa, house wine

vino de la tierra, local wine

vino del país, local wine (wine from the country)

vino de mesa, table wine

vino de Oporto, port

vino de pasto, table wine

vino dulce, dessert wine

vino espumoso, sparkling wine

vino generoso, fortified wine

vino rancio, dessert wine

vino rosado, rosé wine

vino seco, dry wine

vino suave, sweet wine

vino tinto, al, baked in a red-wine sauce

vino tinto, red wine

vino verde, white wine from Galicia

viski, whiskey

viudo de pescado, fish stew

vizcaína, a la, sauce of peppers, onions, paprika, and garlic

vodka, vodka

vuelvealavida, seafood cocktail found in Latin America

whisky, whiskey

whisky americano, bourbon

xai, lamb

xampañ, sparkling wine

xampanyerie, bar found in and around Barcelona serving *cava*
  (sparkling wine)

xampinyons, mushrooms

xató, salad mixed with tomato, olives,
  anchovies and cod or tuna

xatonada, salad mixed with tomato, olives, anchovies and cod or tuna

xerex, another word for *jerez* (sherry)

xocolata, chocolate

ViNo de Oporto.

in case you couldn't figure this out for yourself.

xampañ.

Buen Provicho!

Travel Guides by Andy Herbach

Eating & Drinking Guides

Travel Guides

For a list of all Europe Made Easy travel guides, and to purchase
our books, visit www.eatndrink.com

57711549R00067

Made in the USA
Columbia, SC
12 May 2019